New Perspectives on

MICROSOFT® EXCEL 2000

Brief

JUNE JAMRICH PARSONS

DAN OJA

ROY AGELOFF
University of Rhode Island

COURSE TECHNOLOGY

Thomson Learning™

ONE MAIN STREET, CAMBRIDGE, MA 02142

Australia • Canada • Denmark • Japan • Mexico • New Zealand • Philippines
Puerto Rico • Singapore • South Africa • Spain • United Kingdom • United States

New Perspectives on Microsoft Excel 2000—Brief is published by Course Technology.

Senior Editor	Donna Gridley	**Developmental Editor**	Joan Kalkut
Senior Product Manager	Rachel Crapser	**Production Editor**	Catherine G. DiMassa
Product Manager	Catherine Donaldson	**Text Designer**	Meral Dabcovich
Associate Product Manager	Karen Shortill	**Cover Art Designer**	Douglas Goodman
Editorial Assistant	Melissa Dezotell		

© 2000 by Course Technology, a division of Thomson Learning

For more information contact:

Course Technology
1 Main Street
Cambridge, MA 02142
Or find us on the World Wide Web at: http://www.course.com.

Asia (excluding Japan)
Thomson Learning
60 Albert Street, #15-01
Albert Complex
Singapore 189969

Latin America
Thomson Learning
Seneca, 53
Colonia Polanco
11560 Mexico D.F. Mexico

Japan
Thomson Learning
Palaceside Building 5F
1-1-1 Hitotsubashi, Chiyoda-ku
Tokyo 100 0003 Japan

South Africa
Thomson Learning
Zonnebloem Building,
Constantia Square
526 Sixteenth Road
P.O. Box 2459
Halfway House, 1685
South Africa

Australia/New Zealand
Nelson/Thomson Learning
102 Dodds Street
South Melbourne, Victoria 3205

Canada
Nelson/Thomson Learning
1120 Birchmount Road
Scarborough, Ontario
Canada M1K 5G4

UK/Europe/Middle East
Thomson Learning
Berkshire House
168-173 High Holborn
London
WCIV 7AA United Kingdom

Business Press/Thomson Learning
Berkshire House
168-173 High Holborn
London WCIV 7AA United Kingdom

Thomson Nelson & Sons LTD
Nelson House
Mayfield Road
Walton-on-Thames
KT12 5PL United Kingdom

Spain
Paraninfo/Thomson Learning
Calle Magallanes, 25
28015-MADRID
ESPANA

Distrubution Services
Thomson Learning
Ceriton House
North Way
Andover, Hampshire SP10 5BE

International Headquarters
Thomson Learning
International Division
290 Harbor Drive, 2nd Floor
Stamford, CT 06902-7477

Trademarks

Course Technology and the Open Book logo are registered trademarks and CourseKits is a trademark of Course Technology. Custom Edition is a registered trademark of Thomson Learning.

The Thomson Learning Logo is a registered trademark used herein under license.

Some of the product names and company names used in this book have been used for identification purposes only and may be trademarks or registered trademarks of their respective manufacturers and sellers.

Microsoft and the Office logo are either registered trademarks or trademarks of Microsoft Corporation in the United States and/or other countries. Course Technology is an independent entity from Microsoft Corporation, and not affiliated with Microsoft in any manner. This text may be used in assisting students to prepare for a Microsoft Office User Specialist Exam. Neither Microsoft Corporation, its designated review company, nor Course Technology warrants that use of this text will ensure passing the relevant exam.

Disclaimer

Course Technology reserves the right to revise this publication and make changes from time to time in its content without notice.

ISBN 0-7600-7085-7

Printed in the United States of America

6 7 8 9 10 BM 03 02

PREFACE

The New Perspectives Series

About New Perspectives

Course Technology's **New Perspectives Series** is an integrated system of instruction that combines text and technology products to teach computer concepts, the Internet, and microcomputer applications. Users consistently praise this series for innovative pedagogy, use of interactive technology, creativity, accuracy, and supportive and engaging style.

How is the New Perspectives Series different from other series?

The **New Perspectives Series** distinguishes itself by **innovative technology**, from the renowned Course Labs to the state-of-the-art multimedia that is integrated with our Concepts texts. Other distinguishing features include **sound instructional design, proven pedagogy,** and **consistent quality**. Each tutorial has students learn features in the context of solving a realistic case problem rather than simply learning a laundry list of features. With the **New Perspectives Series,** instructors report that students have a complete, integrative learning experience that stays with them. They credit this high retention and competency to the fact that this series incorporates critical thinking and problem solving with computer skills mastery. In addition, we work hard to ensure accuracy by using a multi-step quality assurance process during all stages of development. Instructors focus on teaching and students spend more time learning.

What course is this book appropriate for?

New Perspectives on Microsoft Excel 2000 — Brief can be used in any course in which you want students to learn the essential topics of Microsoft Excel 2000, including planning and creating a spreadsheet, editing and printing your worksheet, and creating charts. It is particularly recommended for a short course on Excel. This book assumes that students have learned basic Windows 95, 98, NT or Windows 2000 navigation and file management skills from Course Technology's *New Perspectives on Microsoft Windows 95 — Brief*, or the equivalent book for Windows 98, NT, or 2000.

Proven Pedagogy

Tutorial Tips

Tutorial Tips page This page, following the Table of Contents, offers students suggestions on how to effectively plan their study and lab time; what to do when they make a mistake; and how to use the reference windows, MOUS grids, Quick Checks, and other features of the New Perspectives Series.

CASE

Tutorial Case Each tutorial begins with a problem presented in a case that is meaningful to students. The case turns the task of learning how to use an application into a problem-solving process.

45-minute Sessions Each tutorial is divided into sessions that can be completed in about 45 minutes to an hour. Sessions allow instructors to more accurately allocate time in their syllabus, and students to better manage their own study time.

1.
2.
3.

Step-by-Step Methodology We make sure students can differentiate between what they are to *do* and what they are to *read*. Through numbered steps – clearly identified by a gray shaded background – students are constantly guided in solving the case problem. In addition, the numerous screen shots with callouts direct students' attention to what they should look at on the screen.

TROUBLE?

TROUBLE? Paragraphs These paragraphs anticipate the mistakes or problems that students may have and help them continue with the tutorial.

"Read This Before You Begin" Page Located opposite the first tutorial's opening page for each section of the text, the Read This Before You Begin page helps introduce technology into the classroom. Technical considerations and assumptions about software are listed to save time and eliminate unnecessary aggravation. Notes about the Student Disks help instructors and students get the right files in the right places, so students get started on the right foot.

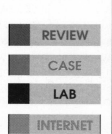

Quick Check Questions Each session concludes with meaningful, conceptual Quick Check questions that test students' understanding of what they learned in the session. Answers to the Quick Check questions are provided at the end of each tutorial.

Reference Windows Reference Windows are succinct summaries of the most important tasks covered in a tutorial and they preview actions students will perform in the steps to follow.

Task Reference Located as a table at the end of the book, the Task Reference contains a summary of how to perform common tasks using the most efficient method, as well as references to pages where the task is discussed in more detail.

End-of-Tutorial Review Assignments, Case Problems, and Lab Assignments Review Assignments provide students with additional hands-on practice of the skills they learned in the tutorial using the same case presented in the tutorial. These Assignments are followed by three to four Case Problems that have approximately the same scope as the tutorial case but use a different scenario. In addition, some of the Review Assignments or Case Problems may include Exploration Exercises that challenge students to explore the capabilities of the program they are using, and/or further extend their knowledge. Each tutorial also includes instructions on getting to the text's Student Online Companion page, which contains the Internet Assignments and other related links for the text. Internet Assignments are additional exercises that integrate the skills the students learned in the tutorial with the World Wide Web. Finally, if a Course Lab accompanies a tutorial, Lab Assignments are included after the Case Problems.

The Instructor's Resource Kit for this title contains:

- Electronic Instructor's Manual in .pdf format
- Student Files
- Solution Files
- Course Test Manager Testbank
- Course Test Manager Engine
- Figure files

These teaching tools come on CD-ROM. If you don't have access to a CD-ROM drive, contact your Course Technology customer service representative for more information.

Acknowledgments

I would like to thank the following reviewers for their excellent feedback: Calleen Coorough, Skagit Valley College; Bonnie Bailey, Moorhead State; Greg Lowry, Mercer University and Macon Technical College; Mary Dobranski, College of St. Mary; and Barbara Miller, Indiana University. Thanks to the dedicated and enthusiastic Course Technology staff, including Melissa Dezotell, Karen Shortill, Rachel Crapser, and Donna Gridley. Thanks as well to all the Production staff, including Catherine DiMassa and everyone from GEX who worked so hard to produce this book. Thanks to John Bosco, Quality Assurance Project leader, and Nicole Ashton, John Freitas, Alex White, Jeff Schwartz — QA testers — for ensuring the accuracy of the text. Special thanks to Joan Kalkut, Developmental Editor.

TABLE OF CONTENTS

Reference Windows List

Tutorial Tips

These tutorials will help you learn about Microsoft Excel 2000. The tutorials are designed to be worked through at a computer. Each tutorial is divided into sessions. Watch for the session headings, such as Session 1.1 and Session 1.2. Each session is designed to be completed in about 45 minutes, but take as much time as you need. It's also a good idea to take a break between sessions.

Before you begin, read the following questions and answers. They will help you plan your time and use the tutorials effectively.

Where do I start?

Each tutorial begins with a case, which sets the scene for the tutorial and gives you background information to help you understand what you will be doing. Read the case before you go to the lab. In the lab, begin with the first session of a tutorial.

How do I know what to do on the computer?

Each session contains steps that you will perform on the computer to learn how to use Microsoft Excel 2000. Read the text that introduces each series of steps. The steps you need to do at a computer are numbered and are set against a shaded background. Read each step carefully and completely before you try it.

How do I know if I did the step correctly?

As you work, compare your computer screen with the corresponding figure in the tutorial. Don't worry if your screen display is somewhat different from the figure. The important parts of the screen display are labeled in each figure. Check to make sure these parts are on your screen.

What if I make a mistake?

Don't worry about making mistakes—they are part of the learning process. Paragraphs labeled "TROUBLE?" identify common problems and explain how to get back on track. Follow the steps in a TROUBLE? paragraph only if you are having the problem described. If you run into other problems:

- Carefully consider the current state of your system, the position of the pointer, and any messages on the screen.

- Complete the sentence, "Now I want to..." Be specific, because identifying your goal will help you rethink the steps you need to take to reach that goal.

- If you are working on a particular piece of software, consult the Help system.

- If the suggestions above don't solve your problem, consult your technical support person for assistance.

How do I use the Reference Windows?

Reference Windows summarize the procedures you will learn in the tutorial steps. Do not complete the actions in the Reference Windows when you are working through the tutorial. Instead, refer to the Reference Windows while you are working on the assignments at the end of the tutorial.

How can I test my understanding of the material I learned in the tutorial?

At the end of each session, you can answer the Quick Check questions. The answers for the Quick Checks are at the end of that tutorial.

After you have completed the entire tutorial, you should complete the Review Assignments and Case Problems. They are carefully structured so that you will review what you have learned and then apply your knowledge to new situations.

What if I can't remember how to do something?

You should refer to the Task Reference at the end of the book; it summarizes how to accomplish tasks using the most efficient method.

Before you begin the tutorials, you should know the basics about your computer's operating system. You should also know how to use the menus, dialog boxes, Help system, and My Computer.

Now that you've read the Tutorial Tips, you are ready to begin.

New Perspectives on

MICROSOFT®
EXCEL 2000

Read This Before You Begin

To the Student

Data Disks

To complete the Level I tutorials, Review Assignments, and Case Problems, you need 2 Data Disks. Your instructor will either provide you with these Data Disks or ask you to make your own.

If you are making your own Data Disks, you will need 2 blank, formatted high-density disks. You will need to copy a set of folders from a file server or standalone computer or the Web onto your disks. Your instructor will tell you which computer, drive letter, and folders contain the files you need. You could also download the files by going to www.course.com, clicking Data Disk Files, and following the instructions on the screen.

The following table shows you which folders go on each of your disks, so that you will have enough disk space to complete all the tutorials, Review Assignments, and Case Problems:

Data Disk 1

Write this on the disk label:
Data Disk 1: Tutorials 1-3

Put these folders and all subfolders on the disk:
Tutorial.01, Tutorial.02, Tutorial.03

Data Disk 2

Write this on the disk label:
Data Disk 2: Tutorial 4

Put these folders and all subfolders on the disk:
Tutorial.04

When you begin each tutorial, be sure you are using the correct Data Disk. Refer to the "File Finder" Chart at the back of this text for more detailed information on which files are used in which tutorials. See the inside front or inside back cover of this book for more information on Data Disk files, or ask your instructor or technical support person for assistance.

Course Labs

The Excel Level I tutorials feature an interactive Course Lab to help you understand spreadsheet concepts. There are Lab Assignments at the end of Tutorial 1 that relate to this Lab.

To start a Lab, click the **Start** button on the Windows taskbar, point to **Programs**, point to **Course Labs**, point to **New Perspectives Course Labs**, and click the name of the Lab you want to use.

Using Your Own Computer

If you are going to work through this book using your own computer, you need:

- **Computer System** Microsoft Windows 95, 98, NT, or higher must be installed on your computer. This book assumes a typical installation of Microsoft Excel.

- **Data Disk** You will not be able to complete the tutorials or exercises in this book using your own computer until you have your Data Disks.

- **Course Labs** See your instructor or technical support person to obtain the Course Lab software for use on your own computer.

Visit Our World Wide Web Site

Additional materials designed especially for you are available on the World Wide Web. Go to http://www.course.com.

To the Instructor

The Data files and Course Labs are available on the Instructor's Resource Kit for this title. Follow the instructions in the Help file on the CD-ROM to install the programs to your network or standalone computer. For information on creating Data Disks or the Course Labs, see the "To the Student" section above.

You are granted a license to copy the Data Files and Course Labs to any computer or computer network used by students who have purchased this book.

OBJECTIVES

In this tutorial you will:

- Start and exit Excel

- Discover how Excel is used in business

- Identify the major components of the Excel window

- Navigate an Excel workbook and worksheet

- Open, save, print, and close a worksheet

- Enter text, numbers, formulas, and functions

- Correct mistakes

- Perform what-if analyses

- Clear contents of cells

- Use the Excel Help system

LABS

Spreadsheets

USING WORKSHEETS TO MAKE BUSINESS DECISIONS

Evaluating Sites for an Inwood Design Group Golf Course

CASE

Inwood Design Group

Golf is big business in Japan. Spurred by the Japanese passion for the sport, golf enjoys unprecedented popularity in Japan. But because the country is small and mountainous, the 12 million golfers have fewer than 2,000 courses from which to choose. Fees for 18 holes on a public course average between $200 and $300; golf club memberships are bought and sold like stock shares. The market potential is phenomenal, but building a golf course in Japan is expensive because of inflated property values, difficult terrain, and strict environmental regulations.

Inwood Design Group plans to build a world-class golf course, and one of the four sites under consideration is Chiba Prefecture, Japan. Other possible sites are Kauai, Hawaii; Edmonton, Canada; and Scottsdale, Arizona. You and Mike Nagochi are members of the site selection team for Inwood. The team is responsible for collecting information on the sites, evaluating that information, and recommending the best site for the new golf course.

Your team identified five factors likely to determine the success of a golf course: Climate, Competition, Market Size, Topography, and Transportation. The team has already collected information on these factors for three of the four potential golf course sites. Mike has just returned from visiting the last site in Scottsdale, Arizona.

Using Microsoft Excel 2000 for Windows, Mike has created a worksheet that the team can use to evaluate the four sites. He needs to complete the worksheet by entering the data for the Scottsdale site. He then plans to bring the worksheet to the group's next meeting so that the team can analyze the information and recommend a site to management.

In this tutorial you will learn how to use Excel as you work with Mike to complete the Inwood site selection worksheet and with the Inwood team to select the best site for the golf course.

SESSION 1.1

In this session you will learn what a spreadsheet is and how it is used in business. You will learn what Excel is and about the Excel window and its elements, how to move around a worksheet using the keyboard and the mouse, and how to open a workbook.

What Is Excel?

Spreadsheets

Excel is a computerized spreadsheet. A **spreadsheet** is an important business tool that helps you analyze and evaluate information. Spreadsheets are often used for cash flow analysis, budgeting, decision making, cost estimating, inventory management, and financial reporting. For example, an accountant might use a spreadsheet like the one in Figure 1-1 for a budget.

Figure 1-1	BUDGET SPREADSHEET

Cash Budget Forecast

	January Estimated	January Actual
Cash in Bank (Start of Month)	$1,400.00	$1,400.00
Cash in Register (Start of Month)	100.00	100.00
Total Cash	$1,500.00	$1,500.00
Expected Cash Sales	$1,200.00	$1,420.00
Expected Collections	400.00	380.00
Other Money Expected	100.00	52.00
Total Income	$1,700.00	$1,852.00
Total Cash and Income	$3,200.00	$3,352.00
All Expenses (for Month)	$1,200.00	$1,192.00
Cash Balance at End of Month	$2,000.00	$2,160.00

To produce the spreadsheet in Figure 1-1, you could manually calculate the totals and then type your results, or you could use a computer and spreadsheet program to perform the calculations and print the results. Spreadsheet programs are also referred to as electronic spreadsheets, computerized spreadsheets, or just spreadsheets.

In Excel 2000, the document you create is called a **workbook**. Each workbook is made up of individual **worksheets**, or **sheets**, just as a spiral-bound notebook is made up of sheets of paper. You will learn more about using multiple sheets later in this tutorial. For now, just keep in mind that the terms *worksheet* and *sheet* are often used interchangeably.

Starting Excel

Mike arrives at his office early because he needs to work with you to finish the worksheet and get ready for your meeting with the design team.

Start Excel and complete the worksheet that Mike will use to help the design team decide about the golf course site.

To start Microsoft Excel:

1. Make sure Windows is running on your computer and the Windows desktop appears on your screen.

2. Click the **Start** button on the taskbar to display the Start menu, and then point to **Programs** to display the Programs menu.

3. Point to **Microsoft Excel** on the Programs menu. See Figure 1-2.

Figure 1-2	STARTING MICROSOFT EXCEL

Office Shortcut Bar (might look different or might not appear on your screen)

position mouse pointer here to display Programs menu

Start button

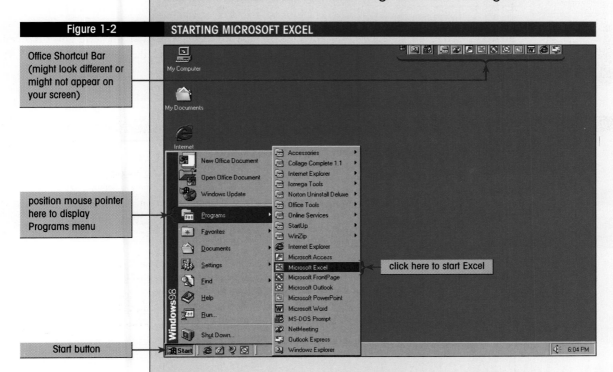

TROUBLE? Don't worry if your screen differs slightly. Although figures in this book were created while running Windows 98 in its default setting, these operating systems share the same basic user interface and Microsoft Excel runs equally well using Windows 95, Windows 98 in Web style, Windows NT, and Windows 2000.

TROUBLE? If the Office Shortcut Bar, which appears along the top border of the desktop in Figure 1-2, looks different on your screen or does not appear at all, your system may be set up differently. The steps in these tutorials do not require that you use the Office Shortcut Bar; therefore, the remaining figures do not display it.

4. Click **Microsoft Excel**. After a short pause, the Microsoft Excel copyright information appears in a message box and remains on the screen until the Excel program window and a blank worksheet appear. See Figure 1-3.

TROUBLE? If the Office Assistant (see Figure 1-3) window opens when you start Excel, click Help on the menu bar then click Hide the Office Assistant. You'll learn more about the Office Assistant later in this tutorial.

| Figure 1-3 | EXCEL PROGRAM WINDOW WITH BLANK WORKSHEET |

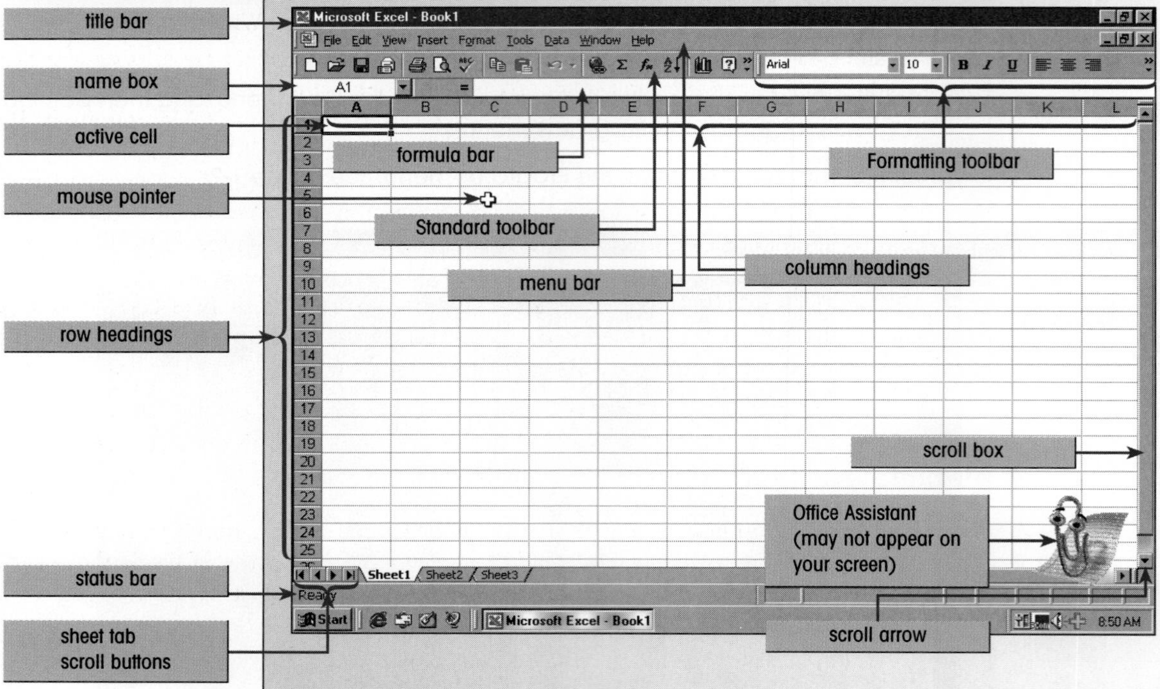

title bar

name box

active cell

mouse pointer

formula bar

Standard toolbar

Formatting toolbar

menu bar

column headings

row headings

scroll box

Office Assistant
(may not appear on
your screen)

status bar

sheet tab
scroll buttons

scroll arrow

5. If the Microsoft Excel program window does not fill the entire screen as in Figure 1-3, click the **Maximize** button ⬜ in the upper-right corner of the program window. If the Book1 window is not maximized, click ⬜ in the upper-right corner of the Book1 window. Your screen should now resemble Figure 1-3.

The Excel Window

The Excel window layout is consistent with the layout of other Windows programs. It contains many common features, such as the title bar, menu bar, scroll bars, and taskbar. Figure 1-3 shows these elements as well as the main components of the Excel window. Take a look at each of these Excel components so you are familiar with their location and purpose.

Toolbars

Toolbars allow you to organize the commands in Excel. The menu bar is a special toolbar at the top of the window that contains menus such as File, Edit, and View. The Standard toolbar and the Formatting toolbar are located below the menu bar. The **Standard** toolbar contains buttons corresponding to the most frequently used commands in Excel. The **Formatting** toolbar contains buttons corresponding to the commands most frequently used to improve the appearance of a worksheet.

Formula Bar

The **formula bar**, located immediately below the toolbars, displays the contents of the active cell. A **cell's contents** is the text, numbers, and formulas you enter into it. As you type or edit data, the changes appear in the formula bar. The **name box** appears at the left end of the formula bar. This area displays the cell reference for the active cell.

Workbook Window

The document window, usually called the **workbook window** or **worksheet window**, contains the sheet you are creating, editing, or using. Each worksheet consists of a series of columns identified by lettered column headings and a series of rows identified by numbered row headings. Columns are assigned alphabetic labels from A to IV (256 columns). Rows are assigned numeric labels from 1 to 65,536 (65,536 rows).

A **cell** is the rectangular area where a column and a row intersect. Each cell is identified by a **cell reference**, which is its column and row location. For example, the cell reference B6 indicates the cell where column B and row 6 intersect. The column letter is always first in the cell reference. B6 is a correct cell reference; 6B is not. The **active cell** is the cell in which you are currently working. Excel identifies the active cell with a dark border that outlines one cell. In Figure 1-3, cell A1 is the active cell. Notice that the cell reference for the active cell appears in the name box of the formula bar. You can change the active cell when you want to work elsewhere in the worksheet.

Pointer

The **pointer** is the indicator that moves on your screen as you move your mouse. The pointer changes shape to reflect the type of task you can perform at a particular location. When you click a mouse button, something happens at the pointer's location. In Figure 1-3, the pointer looks like a white plus sign ✛.

Sheet Tabs

Each worksheet has a **sheet tab** that identifies the name of the worksheet. The name on the tab of the active sheet is bold. The sheet tabs let you move quickly between the sheets in a workbook; you can simply check the sheet tab of the sheet you want to move to. By default, a new workbook consists of three worksheets. If your workbook contains many worksheets, you can use the **sheet tab scroll buttons** to scroll through the sheet tabs that are not currently visible to find the sheet you want.

Moving Around a Worksheet

Before entering or editing the contents of a cell, you need to select that cell to make it the active cell. You can select a cell using either the keyboard or the mouse.

Using the Mouse

Using the mouse, you can quickly select a cell by placing the mouse pointer on the cell and clicking the mouse button. If you need to move to a cell that's not currently on the screen, use the vertical and horizontal scroll bars to display the area of the worksheet containing the cell you are interested in, and then select the cell.

Using the Keyboard

In addition to the mouse, Excel provides you with many keyboard options for moving to different cell locations within your worksheet. Figure 1-4 shows some of the keys you can use to select a cell within your worksheet.

Figure 1-4	KEYS TO MOVE AROUND THE WORKSHEET
KEYSTROKE	**ACTION**
↑, ↓, ←, →	Moves up, down, left, or right one cell
PgUp	Moves the active cell up one full screen
PgDn	Moves the active cell down one full screen
Home	Moves the active cell to column A of the current row
Ctrl + Home	Moves the active cell to cell A1
F5 (function key)	Opens Go To dialog box, in which you enter cell address of cell you want to make active cell

Now, try moving around the worksheet using your keyboard and mouse.

To move around the worksheet:

1. Position the mouse pointer ⊕ over cell E8, then click the **left mouse** button to make it the active cell. Notice that the cell is surrounded by a black border to indicate that it is the active cell and that the name box on the formula bar displays E8.

2. Click cell **B4** to make it the active cell.

3. Press the → key to make cell C4 the active cell.

4. Press the ↓ key to make cell C5 the active cell. See Figure 1-5.

Figure 1-5	CELL C5 AS ACTIVE CELL

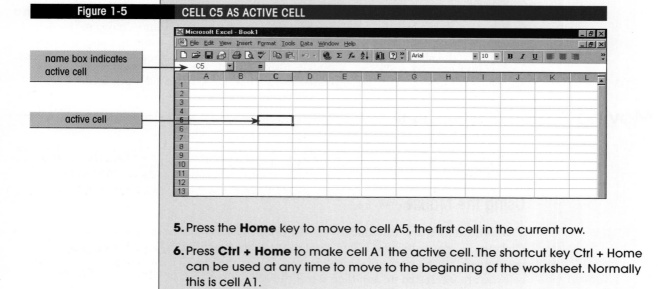

name box indicates active cell

active cell

5. Press the **Home** key to move to cell A5, the first cell in the current row.

6. Press **Ctrl + Home** to make cell A1 the active cell. The shortcut key Ctrl + Home can be used at any time to move to the beginning of the worksheet. Normally this is cell A1.

So far you've moved around the portion of the worksheet you can see. Many worksheets can't be viewed entirely on one screen. Next, you'll use the keyboard and mouse to bring other parts of the worksheet into view.

To bring other parts of the worksheet into view:

1. Press the **Page Down** key to move the display down one screen. The active cell is now cell A26 (the active cell on your screen may be different). Notice that the row numbers on the left side of the worksheet indicate you have moved to a different area of the worksheet. See Figure 1-6.

| Figure 1-6 | WORKSHEET SCREEN AFTER MOVING TO DIFFERENT AREA OF WORKSHEET |

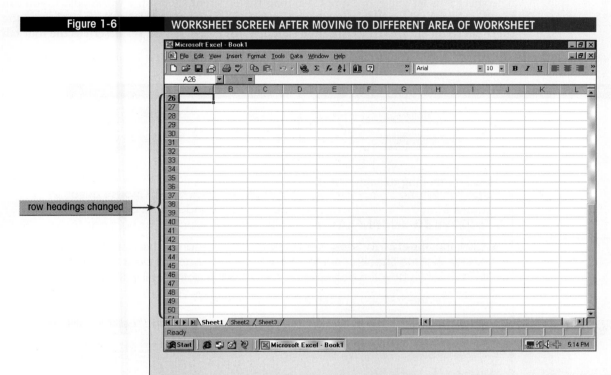

row headings changed

2. Press the **Page Down** key again to move the display down one screen. Notice that the row numbers indicate that you have moved to a different area of the worksheet.

3. Press the **Page Up** key to move the display up one screen. The active cell is now cell A26 (the active cell on your screen may be different).

4. Click the **vertical scroll bar up arrow** button until row 12 is visible. Notice that the active cell is still A26 (the active cell on your screen may be different). Using the scroll bar changes the portion of the screen you can view without changing the active cell.

5. Click cell **C12** to make it the active cell.

6. Click the blank area above the vertical scroll box to move up a full screen.

7. Click the blank area below the vertical scroll box to move down a full screen.

8. Click the **scroll box** and drag it to the top of the scroll area to again change the area of the screen you're viewing. Notice that the ScrollTip appears telling you the current row location.

9. Press **F5** to open the Go To dialog box.

10. Type **K55** in the Reference box and then click **OK**. Cell K55 is now the active cell.

11. Press **Ctrl + Home** to make cell A1 the active cell. Now click cell **E6**.

As you know, a workbook can consist of one or more worksheets. Excel makes it easy to switch between them. Next, try moving from worksheet to worksheet.

Navigating in a Workbook

The sheet tabs let you move quickly among the different sheets in a workbook. If you can see the tab of the sheet you want, click the tab to activate the worksheet. You can also use the sheet tab scroll buttons to see sheet tabs hidden from view. Figure 1-7 describes the four tab scrolling buttons and their effects.

Figure 1-7	SHEET TAB SCROLLING BUTTONS

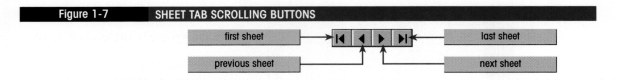

Next, try moving to a new sheet.

To move to Sheet2:

1. Click the **Sheet2** tab. Sheet2, which is blank, appears in the worksheet window. Notice that the Sheet2 sheet tab is white and the name is bold, which means that Sheet2 is now the active sheet. Cell A1 is the active cell in Sheet2.

2. Click the **Sheet3** tab to make it the active sheet.

3. Click the **Sheet1** tab to make it the active sheet. Notice that cell E6 is still the active cell.

Now that you have some basic skills navigating a worksheet and workbook, you can begin working with Mike to complete the golf site selection worksheet.

Opening a Workbook

When you want to use a workbook that you previously created, you must first open it. Opening a workbook transfers a copy of the workbook file from the hard drive or 3½-inch disk to the random access memory (RAM) of your computer and displays it on your screen. When the workbook is open, the file is both in RAM and on the disk.

After you open a workbook, you can view, edit, print, or save it again on your disk.

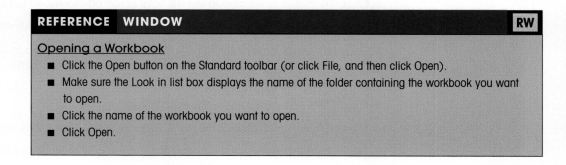

REFERENCE WINDOW   **RW**

Opening a Workbook
- Click the Open button on the Standard toolbar (or click File, and then click Open).
- Make sure the Look in list box displays the name of the folder containing the workbook you want to open.
- Click the name of the workbook you want to open.
- Click Open.

Mike created a workbook to help the site selection team evaluate the four potential locations for the golf course. The workbook, Inwood, is on your Data Disk.

To open an existing workbook:

1. Place your Excel Data Disk in the appropriate drive.

TROUBLE? If you don't have a Data Disk, you need to get one before you can proceed. Your instructor or technical support person will either give you one or ask you to make your own by following the instructions on the "Read This Before You Begin" page before this tutorial. See your instructor or technical support person for information.

2. Click the **Open** button 📂 on the Standard toolbar. The Open dialog box opens. See Figure 1-8.

Figure 1-8	OPEN DIALOG BOX

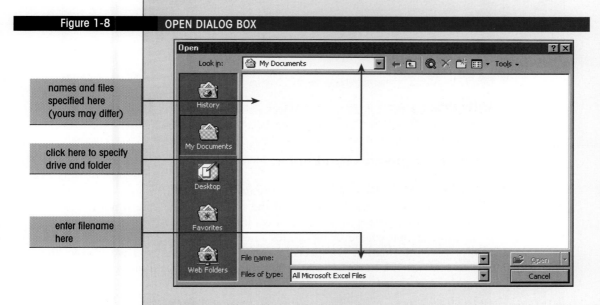

names and files specified here (yours may differ)

click here to specify drive and folder

enter filename here

3. Click the **Look in** list arrow to display the list of available drives. Locate the drive containing your Data Disk. In this text, we assume your Data Disk is a 3½-inch disk in drive A.

4. Click the drive that contains your Data Disk. A list of documents and folders on your Data Disk appears in the list box.

5. In the list of document and folder names, double-click **Tutorial.01,** double-click **Tutorial** to display that folder in the Look in list box, then click **Inwood**.

6. Click the **Open** button 📂. (You could also double-click the filename to open the file.) The Inwood workbook opens and the first sheet in the workbook, Documentation, appears. See Figure 1-9. Notice the filename, Inwood, appears on the title bar at the top of your screen.

Figure 1-9	DOCUMENTATION SHEET IN INWOOD WORKBOOK

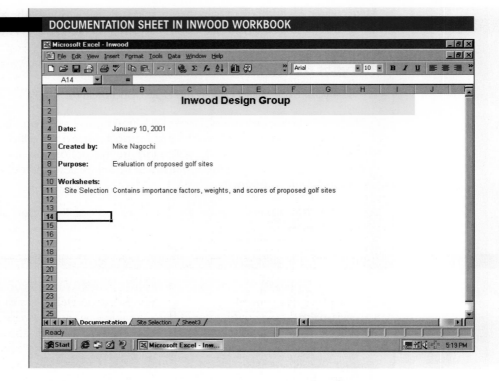

Layout of the Inwood Workbook

The first worksheet, Documentation, contains information about the workbook. The Documentation sheet shows who created the workbook, the date when it was created, its purpose, and a brief description of each sheet in the workbook.

Mike explains that whenever he creates a new workbook he makes sure he documents it carefully. This information is especially useful if he returns to a workbook after a long period of time (or if a new user opens it) because it provides a quick review of the workbook's purpose.

After reviewing the Documentation sheet, Mike moves to the Site Selection worksheet.

To move to the Site Selection worksheet:

1. Click the **Site Selection** sheet tab to display the worksheet Mike is preparing for the site selection team. See Figure 1-10.

Figure 1-10   **SITE SELECTION WORKSHEET**

Microsoft Excel - Inwood

File Edit View Insert Format Tools Data Window Help

	A	B	C	D	E	F	G	H	I
1	Factor	Importance		Raw Scores					
2		Weight	Kauai	Edmonton	Chiba				
3	Climate	8	5	1	4				
4	Competition	7	3	5	4				
5	Market Size	10	3	4	5				
6	Topography	7	4	4	1				
7	Transportation	5	2	3	4				
8									
9		Criteria		Weighted Scores					
10			Kauai	Edmonton	Chiba				
11		Climate	40	8	32				
12		Competition	21	35	28				
13		Market Size	30	40	50				
14		Topography	28	28	7				
15		Transportation	10	15	20				
16			Kauai	Edmonton	Chiba				
17		*Total*	129	126	137				
18									

Mike explains the general layout of the Site Selection worksheet to you. He reminds you that to this point he has only entered data for three of the four sites. He will provide the missing Scottsdale information to you. Cells C2 through E2 list three of the four sites for which he has data. Cells A3 through A7 contain the five factors on which the team's decision will be based: Climate, Competition, Market Size, Topography, and Transportation. They assign scores for Climate, Competition, Market Size, Topography, and Transportation to each location. The team uses a scale of 1 to 5 to assign a raw score for each factor. Higher raw scores indicate strength; lower raw scores indicate weakness. Cells C3 through E7 contain the raw scores for the first three locations. For example, the raw score for Kauai's Climate is 5; the two other locations have scores of 1 and 4, so Kauai, with its warm, sunny days all year, has the best climate for the golf course of the three sites visited so far. Edmonton, on the other hand, has cold weather and only received a Climate raw score of 1.

The raw scores, however, do not provide enough information for the team to make a decision. Some factors are more important to the success of the golf course than others. The team members assigned an *importance weight* to each factor according to their knowledge of what factors contribute most to the success of a golf course. The importance weights are on a scale from 1 to 10, with 10 being most important. Mike entered the weights in cells B3 through B7. Market size, weighted 10, is the most important factor. The team believes the least important factor is Transportation, so Transportation is assigned a lower weight. Climate is important but the team considers Market Size most important. They do not use the raw scores to make a final decision; instead, they multiply each raw score by its importance weight to produce a weighted score. Which of the three sites already visited has the highest weighted score for any factor? If you look at the scores in cells C11 through E15, you see that Chiba's score of 50 for Market Size is the highest weighted score for any factor.

Cells C17 through E17 contain the total weighted scores for the three locations. With the current weighted and raw scores, Chiba is the most promising site, with a total score of 137.

Session 1.1 QUICK CHECK

1. A(n) _____ is the rectangular area where a column and a row intersect.

2. When you _____ a workbook, the computer copies it from your disk into RAM.

3. The cell reference _____ refers to the intersection of the fourth column and the second row.

4. To move the worksheet to the right one column:

   a. press the Enter key
   b. click the right arrow on the horizontal scroll bar
   c. press the Esc key
   d. press Ctrl + Home

5. To make Sheet2 the active worksheet, you would _____.

6. What key or keys do you press to make cell A1 the active cell?

You have now reviewed the layout of the worksheet. Now, Mike wants you to enter the data on Scottsdale. Based on his meeting with local investors and a visit to the Scottsdale site, he has assigned the following raw scores: Climate 5, Competition 2, Market Size 4, Topography 3, and Transportation 3. To complete the worksheet, you must enter the raw scores he has assigned to the Scottsdale site. You will do this in the next session.

SESSION 1.2

In this session you will learn how to enter text, values, formulas, and functions into a worksheet. You will use this data to perform what-if analyses using a worksheet. You'll also correct mistakes and use the online Help system to determine how to clear the contents of cells. Finally, you'll learn how to print a worksheet and how to close a worksheet and exit Excel.

Text, Values, Formulas, and Functions

As you have now observed, an Excel workbook can hold one or more worksheets, each containing a grid of 256 columns and 65,536 rows. The rectangular areas at the intersections of each column and row are called cells. A cell can contain a value, text, or a formula. To understand how the spreadsheet program works, you need to understand how Excel manipulates text, values, formulas, and functions.

Text

Text entries include any combination of letters, symbols, numbers, and spaces. Although text is sometimes used as data, it is more often used to describe the data contained in a worksheet. Text is often used to label columns and rows in a worksheet. For example, a projected monthly income statement contains the months of the year as column headings and income and expense categories as row labels. To enter text in a worksheet, you select the cell in which you want to enter the text by clicking the cell to select it, then typing the text. Excel automatically aligns the text on the left in a cell.

Mike's Site Selection worksheet contains a number of column heading labels. You need to enter the label for Scottsdale in the Raw Scores and Weighted Scores sections of the worksheet.

To enter a text label:

1. If you took a break after the last session, make sure Excel is running and make sure the Site Selection worksheet of the Inwood workbook is showing.

2. Click cell **F2** to make it the active cell.

3. Type **Scottsdale**, then press the **Enter** key.

    TROUBLE? If you make a mistake while typing, you can correct the error with the Backspace key. If you realize you made an error after you press the Enter key, retype the entry by repeating Steps 2 and 3.

4. Click cell **F10** and type **S**. Excel completes the entry for you based on the entries already in the column. If your data involves repetitious text, this feature, known as **AutoComplete**, can make your data entry go more quickly.

5. Press the **Enter** key to complete the entry.

6. Click cell **F16**, type **S**, and press the **Enter** key to accept Scottsdale as the entry in the cell. See Figure 1-11. Next, you need to enter the raw scores Mike assigned to Scottsdale.

Figure 1-11	WORKSHEET AFTER TEXT HAS BEEN ENTERED

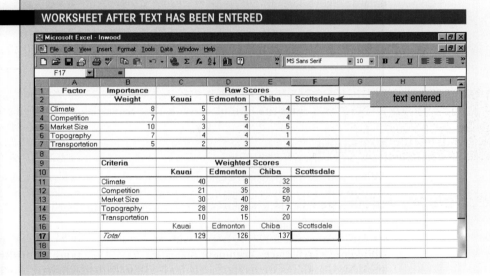

Values

Values are numbers that represent a quantity of some type: the number of units in inventory, stock price, an exam score, and so on. Examples of values are 378, 25.275, and -55. Values can also be dates (11/29/99) and times (4:40:31). As you type information in a cell, Excel determines whether the characters you're typing can be used as values. For example, if you type 456, Excel recognizes it as a value and it is right-justified in the cell. On the other hand, Excel treats some data commonly referred to as "numbers" as text. For example, Excel treats a telephone number (1-800-227-1240) or a Social Security number (372-70-9654) as text that cannot be used for calculations.

You need to enter the raw scores for Scottsdale.

To enter a value:

1. If necessary, click the scroll arrow so row 2 is visible. Click cell **F3**, type **5** and then press the **Enter** key. The active cell is now cell F4.

2. With cell F4 as the active cell, type **2** and press the **Enter** key.

3. Enter the value **4** for Market Size in cell F5, the value **3** for Topography in cell F6, and the value **3** for Transportation in cell F7. See Figure 1-12.

Figure 1-12	WORKSHEET AFTER NUMBERS HAVE BEEN ENTERED

Next, you enter the formulas to calculate Scottsdale's weighted score in each category.

Formulas

When you need to perform a calculation in Excel you use a formula. A **formula** is the arithmetic used to calculate values appearing in a worksheet. You can take advantage of the power of Excel by using formulas in worksheets. If you change one number in a worksheet, Excel recalculates any formula affected by the change.

An Excel formula always begins with an equal sign (=). Formulas are created by combining numbers, cell references, arithmetic operators, and/or functions. An **arithmetic operator** indicates the desired arithmetic operations. Figure 1-13 shows the arithmetic operators used in Excel.

Figure 1-13	ARITHMETIC OPERATORS USED IN FORMULAS

ARITHMETIC OPERATIONS	ARITHMETIC OPERATOR	EXAMPLE	DESCRIPTION
Addition	+	=10+A5 =B1+B2+B3	Adds 10 to value in cell A5 Adds the values of cells B1, B2, and B3
Subtraction	−	=C9−B2 =1−D2	Subtracts the value in cell B2 from the value in cell C9 Subtracts the value in cell D2 from 1
Multiplication	*	=C9*B9 =E5*.06	Multiplies the value in cell C9 by the value in cell B9 Multiplies the value in E5 by the constant .06
Division	/	=C9/B9 =D15/12	Divides the value in cell C9 by the value in cell B9 Divides the value in cell D15 by 12
Exponentiation	^	=B5^3 =3^B5	Raises the value stored in cell B5 to 3 Raises 3 to the value stored in cell B5

The result of the formula appears in the cell where you entered the formula. To view the formula that has been entered in a cell, you must first select the cell, then look at the formula bar.

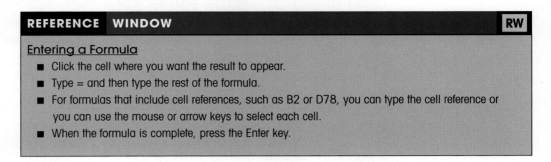

REFERENCE WINDOW   **RW**

Entering a Formula
- Click the cell where you want the result to appear.
- Type = and then type the rest of the formula.
- For formulas that include cell references, such as B2 or D78, you can type the cell reference or you can use the mouse or arrow keys to select each cell.
- When the formula is complete, press the Enter key.

You need to enter the formulas to compute the weighted scores for the Scottsdale site. The formula multiples the raw score for a factor by the importance weight assigned to the factor. Figure 1-14 displays the formulas you need to enter into the worksheet.

Figure 1-14	FORMULAS TO CALCULATE SCOTTSDALE'S WEIGHTED SCORES	
CELL	**FORMULA**	**EXPLANATION**
F11	=B3*F3	Multiplies importance weight by raw score for Climate
F12	=B4*F4	Multiplies importance weight by raw score for Competition
F13	=B5*F5	Multiplies importance weight by raw score for Market Size
F14	=B6*F6	Multiplies importance weight by raw score for Topography
F15	=B7*F7	Multiplies importance weight by raw score for Transportation

To enter the formulas to calculate each weighted score for the Scottsdale site:

1. Click cell **F11** to make it the active cell. Type **=B3*F3** to multiply the weight assigned to the Climate category by the raw score assigned to Scottsdale for the Climate category. Press the **Enter** key. The value 40 appears in cell F11.

   TROUBLE? If you make a mistake while typing, you can correct the error with the Backspace key. If you realize you made an error after you press the Enter key, repeat Step 1 to retype the entry.

2. Click cell **F11** to make it the active cell again. See Figure 1-15. Notice, the results of the formula appear in the cell, but the formula you entered appears on the formula bar.

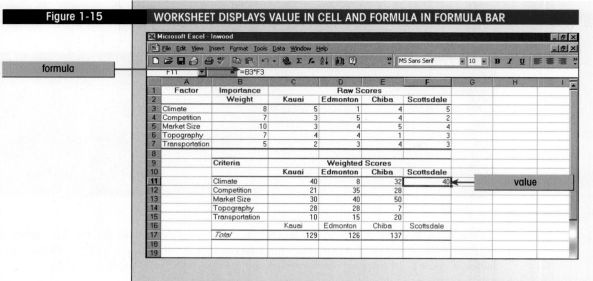

Figure 1-15   WORKSHEET DISPLAYS VALUE IN CELL AND FORMULA IN FORMULA BAR

3. Click cell **F12**, type **=B4*F4**, and then press the **Enter** key. This formula multiplies the weight assigned to Competition (the contents of cell B4) by Scottsdale's raw score for Competition (cell F4). The value 14 appears in cell F12.

4. Enter the remaining formulas from Figure 1-14 into cells F13, F14, and F15. When completed, your worksheet will contain the values 40, 14, 40, 21, and 15 in cells F11 to F15.

TROUBLE? If any value in cells F11 through F15 differs, retype the formula for that cell.

You now have to enter the formula to calculate the total weighted score for Scottsdale into the worksheet. You can use the formula =F11+F12+F13+F14+F15 to calculate the total score for the Scottsdale site. As an alternative, you can use a function to streamline this long formula.

Functions

A **function** is a predefined or built-in formula that's a shortcut for commonly used calculations. For example, the SUM function is a shortcut for entering formulas that total values in rows or columns. You can use the SUM function to create the formula =SUM(F11:F15) instead of typing the longer =F11+F12+F13+F14+F15. The SUM function in this example adds the range F11 through F15. A **range** is a group of cells, either a single cell or a rectangular block of cells. The range reference F11:F15 in the function SUM(F11:F15) refers to the rectangular block of cells beginning in the upper-left corner (F11) and ending in the lower-right corner (F15) of the range. The colon separates the upper-left corner and lower-right corner of the range. Figure 1-16 shows several examples of ranges.

Figure 1-19   **SAVING THE WORKSHEET WITH A NEW FILENAME**

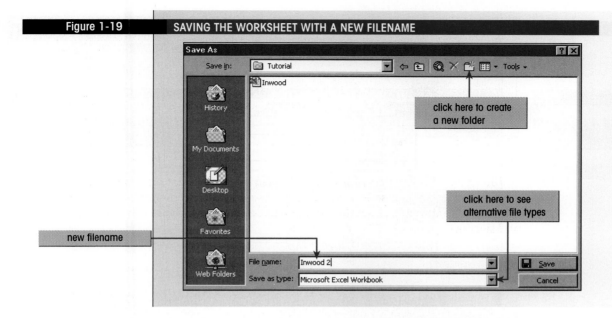

You now have two versions of the workbook: the original file—Inwood—and the modified workbook—Inwood 2.

What-if **Analysis**

The worksheet for site selection is now complete. Mike is ready to show it to the group. As the team examines the worksheet, you ask if the raw scores take into account recent news that a competing design group has announced plans to build a $325-million golf resort just 10 miles away from Inwood's proposed site in Chiba. Mike admits that he assigned the values before the announcement, so the raw scores do not reflect the increased competition in the Chiba market. You suggest revising the raw score for the Competition factor to reflect this market change in Chiba.

When you change a value in a worksheet, Excel automatically recalculates the worksheet and displays updated results. The recalculation feature makes Excel an extremely useful decision-making tool because it lets you quickly and easily factor in changing conditions. When you revise the contents of one or more cells in a worksheet and observe the effect this change has on all the other cells, you are performing a **what-if analysis**. In effect, you are saying, what if I change the value assigned to this factor? What effect will it have on the outcomes in the worksheet?

Because another development group has announced plans to construct a new golf course in the Chiba area, the team decides to lower Chiba's Competition raw score from 4 to 2.

To change Chiba's Competition raw score from 4 to 2:

1. Click cell **E4**. The black border around cell E4 indicates that it is the active cell. The current value of cell E4 is 4.

2. Type **2**. Notice that 2 appears in the cell and in the formula bar, along with a formula palette of three new buttons. The buttons shown in Figure 1-20—the Cancel button ☒, the Enter button ☑, and the Edit Formula button ▣ offer alternatives for canceling, entering, and editing data and formulas.

Figure 1-20   **CHANGING A CELL'S CONTENTS**

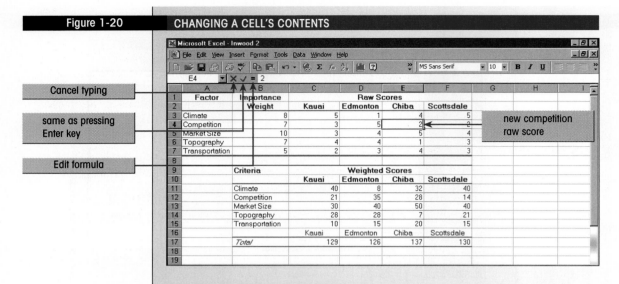

Cancel typing

same as pressing
Enter key

Edit formula

new competition
raw score

3. Click the **Enter** button. Excel recalculates Chiba's weighted score for the Competition factor (cell E12) and the total score for Chiba (cell E17). If necessary, click the **vertical scroll** arrow until row 17 is visible on your screen. The recalculated values are 14 and 123. See Figure 1-21.

Figure 1-21   **WORKSHEET AFTER FORMULAS ARE RECALCULATED**

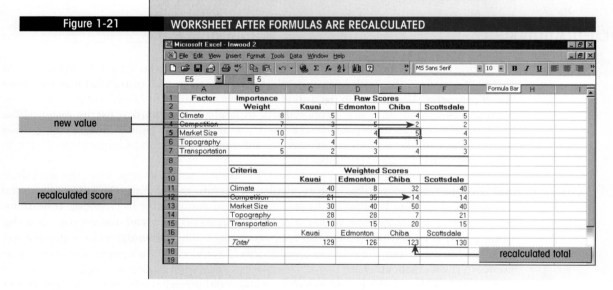

new value

recalculated score

recalculated total

The team takes another look at the total weighted scores in row 17. Scottsdale is now the top-ranking site, with a total weighted score of 130, compared to Chiba's total weighted score of 123.

As the team continues to discuss the worksheet, several members express concern over the importance weight used for Transportation. In the current worksheet, Transportation is weighted 5 (cell B7). You remember that the group agreed to use an importance weight of 2 at a previous meeting. You ask Mike to change the importance weight for Transportation.

To change the importance weight for Transportation:

1. Click cell **B7** to make it the active cell.

2. Type **2** and press the **Enter** key. Cell B7 now contains the value 2 instead of 5. Cell B8 becomes the active cell. See Figure 1-22. Notice that the weighted scores for Transportation (row 15) and the total weighted scores for each site (row 17) have all changed.

| Figure 1-22 | WORKSHEET AFTER CHANGE MADE TO THE TRANSPORTATION IMPORTANCE WEIGHT |

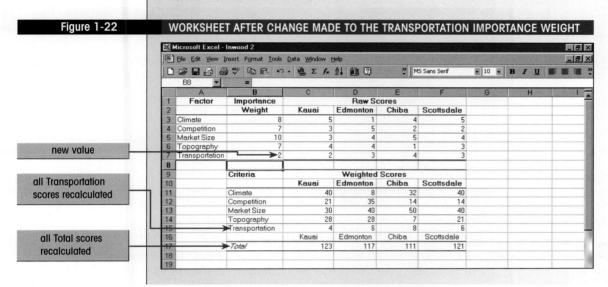

new value

all Transportation scores recalculated

all Total scores recalculated

The change in the Transportation importance weight puts Kauai ahead as the most favorable site, with a total weighted score of 123.

As you enter and edit a worksheet, there are many data entry errors that can occur. The most commonly made mistake on a worksheet is a typing error. Typing mistakes are easy to correct.

Correcting Mistakes

It is easy to correct a mistake as you are typing information in a cell, before you press the Enter key. If you need to correct a mistake as you are typing information in a cell, press the Backspace key to back up and delete one or more characters. If you want to start over, press the Esc key to cancel all changes. When you are typing information in a cell, *don't* use the cursor arrow keys to edit because they move the cell pointer to another cell. One of the team members suggests changing the label "Criteria" in cell B9 to "Factors." The team members agree and you make the change to the cell.

To correct a mistake as you type:

1. Click cell **B9** to make it the active cell.

2. Type **Fak**, intentionally making an error, but don't press the Enter key.

3. Press the **Backspace** key to delete "k".

4. Type **ctors** and press the **Enter** key.

Now the word "Factors" is in cell B9. Mike suggests changing "Factors" to "Factor." The team agrees. To change a cell's contents after you press the Enter key, you use a different method. You can either retype the contents of a cell, or enter Edit mode to change the contents of a cell on the formula bar. Double-clicking a cell or pressing the F2 key puts Excel into **Edit** mode, which lets you use the Home, End, Delete, Backspace keys and the ← and → keys, and the mouse to change the text in the formula bar.

REFERENCE   WINDOW   **RW**

Correcting Mistakes Using Edit Mode

■ Double-click the cell you want to edit to begin Edit mode. The contents of the cell appear directly in the cell as well as the formula bar (or click the cell you want to edit, then press F2).

■ Use Home, End, Delete, Backspace, ←, → or the mouse to edit the cell's contents either in the cell or in the formula bar.

■ Press the Enter key when you finish editing.

You use Edit mode to change "Factors" to "Factor" in cell B9.

To change the word "Factors" to "Factor" in cell B9:

1. Double-click cell **B9** to begin Edit mode. Note that "Edit" appears in the status bar, reminding you that Excel is currently in Edit mode.

2. Press the **End** key if necessary to move the cursor to the right of the word "Factors," then press the **Backspace** key to delete the "s".

3. Press the **Enter** key to complete the edit.

You ask if the team is ready to recommend a site. Mike believes that, based on the best information they have, Kauai should be the recommended site and Scottsdale the alternative site. You ask for a vote, and the team unanimously agrees with Mike's recommendation.

Mike wants to have complete documentation to accompany the team's written recommendation to management, so he wants to print the worksheet.

As he reviews the worksheet one last time, he thinks that the labels in cells C16 through F16 (Kauai, Edmonton, Chiba, Scottsdale) are unnecessary and decides he wants you to delete them before printing the worksheet. You ask how to delete the contents of a cell or a group of cells. Mike is not sure, so he suggests using the Excel Help system to find the answer.

Getting Help

If you don't know how to perform a task or forget how to carry out a particular task, Excel provides an extensive on-screen help. The Excel Help system provides the same options as the Help system in other Office programs—asking help from the Office Assistant, getting help from the Help menu, and obtaining help information from Microsoft's web site. If you are not connected to the Web, you only have access to the Help files stored on your computer.

One way to get help is to use the Office Assistant, which you may have seen on your screen when you first started Excel, and which you closed earlier in this tutorial. The Office Assistant, an animated object, pops up on the screen when you click the Microsoft Excel

Figure 1-29   **PRINTED WORKSHEET**

Factor	Importance Weight	Raw Scores			
		Kauai	Edmonton	Chiba	Scottsdale
Climate	8	5	1	4	5
Competition	7	3	5	2	2
Market Size	10	3	4	5	4
Topography	7	4	4	1	3
Transportation	2	2	3	4	3

Factor	Weighted Scores			
	Kauai	Edmonton	Chiba	Scottsdale
Climate	40	8	32	40
Competition	21	35	14	14
Market Size	30	40	50	40
Topography	28	28	7	21
Transportation	4	6	8	6
Total	123	117	111	121

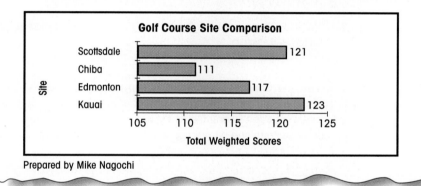

Prepared by Mike Nagochi

Mike volunteers to put together the report with the team's final recommendation, and the meeting adjourns. You and Mike are finished working with the worksheet and are ready to close the workbook.

Closing the Workbook

Closing a workbook removes it from the screen. If a workbook contains changes that have not been saved, Excel asks if you want to save your modified worksheet before closing the workbook. You can now close the workbook.

To close the Inwood 2 workbook:

1. Click **File** on the menu bar, and then click **Close**. A dialog box displays the message "Do you want to save the changes you made to 'Inwood 2.xls'?" Click Yes, if you want to save the changes you made since last saving the workbook. Click No, if you do not want to keep the changes you've made to the workbook.

2. Click **Yes** to save the Inwood 2 workbook before closing it.

The Excel window stays open so you can open or create another workbook. You do not want to, so your next step is to exit Excel.

Exiting Excel

To exit Excel, you can click the Close button on the title bar, or you can use the Exit command on the File menu.

To exit Excel:

1. Click the **Close** button ☒ on the title bar. Excel closes and you return to the Windows desktop.

The Inwood site selection team has completed its work. Mike's worksheet helped the team analyze the data and recommend Kauai as the best site for Inwood's next golf course. Although the Japanese market was a strong factor in favor of locating the course in Japan's Chiba Prefecture, the mountainous terrain and competition from nearby courses reduced the site's desirability.

Session 1.2 QUICK CHECK

1. Indicate whether Excel treats the following cell entries as a value, text, or a formula:

   a. 11/09/2001   **e.** 200-19-1121
   b. Net Income   **f.** D1-D9
   c. 321   **g.** 44 Evans Avenue
   d. =C11*225

2. You type a character and Excel finishes the entry based on entries already in the column. This feature is known as _____.

3. The formula =SUM(C3:I3) adds how many cells? Write an equivalent formula without using the SUM function.

4. What cells are included in the range D5:G7?

5. Why do you need to save a worksheet? What command do you use to save the worksheet?

6. Explain the term *what-if analysis*.

7. You can get Excel Help in any of the following ways except:

   a. clicking Help on the menu bar
   b. clicking the Help button on the Standard toolbar
   c. closing the program window
   d. pressing the F1 key

8. What key do you press to clear the contents of an active cell?

9. To print a copy of your worksheet, you use the _____ command on the _____ menu.

REVIEW ASSIGNMENTS

The other company that had planned a golf course in Chiba, Japan, has run into financial difficulties. Rumors are that the project may be canceled. A copy of the final Inwood Design Group workbook is on your Data Disk. Do the Tutorial Assignments to change this worksheet to show how the cancellation of the other project will affect your site selection.

1. If necessary, start Excel and make sure your Data Disk is in the appropriate disk drive. Open the **Inwood 3** file in the Review folder for Tutorial.01 on your Data Disk.

2. Use the Save As command to save the workbook as **Inwood 4** in the Review folder for Tutorial 1. That way you won't change the original workbook.

3. In the Site Selection worksheet, change the competition raw score for Chiba from 2 to 4. What site is ranked first?

4. The label "Topography" in cell A8 was entered incorrectly as "Topogriphy." Use Edit mode to change the "i" to "a".

5. Enter the text "Scores if the competing project in Chiba, Japan, is canceled" in cell A1.

6. Remove the raw scores for Chiba, cells E5 through E9.

7. Type your name in cell A42, then save the worksheet.

8. Print the worksheet.

9. Print the worksheet data without the chart. (*Hint*: Select the worksheet data before checking out the options in the Print dialog box.)

10. Use the What's This button [?]. Learn more about the following Excel window components:
   a. Name box
   b. Sheet tabs
   c. Tab scrolling button (*Hint*: Click [?], then click each item with the Help pointer.)

11. Use the Office Assistant to learn how to delete a sheet from a workbook. Write the steps to delete a sheet. Delete Sheet3.

12. In addition to the Office Assistant, Excel offers a Help window with three sections of Help: Contents, Index, and Answer Wizard. Use the Contents tab from Microsoft Excel Help window to learn how to insert an additional worksheet into your workbook. (*Hint*: Choose Working in workbooks.) Write the steps to insert a worksheet.

13. Close the workbook and exit Excel without saving the changes.

CASE PROBLEMS

Case 1. ***Enrollments in the University*** You work 10 hours a week in the provost's office at your college. The assistant to the provost has a number of meetings today and has asked you to complete a worksheet she needs for a meeting with college deans this afternoon.

1. Open the workbook **Enroll** in the Cases folder for Tutorial.01 on your Data Disk.

2. Use the Save As command to save the workbook as **Enrollment**.

3. Complete the workbook by performing the following tasks:

   a. Enter the title "Enrollment Data for University" in cell A1.
   b. Enter the label "Total" in cell A9.
   c. Calculate the total enrollment in the University for 2001 in cell B9.
   d. Calculate the total enrollment in the University for 2000 in cell C9.
   e. Calculate the change in enrollments from 2000 to 2001. Place the results in column D. Label the column heading "Change" and use the following formula:

      Change = 2001 enrollment – 2000 enrollment

4. Type "Prepared by [your name]" in cell A12.

5. Save the workbook.

6. Print the worksheet.

Case 2. Cash Budgeting at Halpern's Appliances   Fran Valence, the business manager for Halpern's Appliances, a retail appliance store, is preparing a cash budget for January. The store has a loan that must be paid the first week in February. Fran wants to determine whether the business will have enough cash to make the loan payment to the bank.

Fran sketches the projected budget so that it will have the format shown in Figure 1-30.

Figure 1-30

```
            Halpern's Appliances Cash Budget
         Projected Cash Receipts and Disbursements
         January 1, 2001
         Cash balance, January 1, 2001                        xxxx
         Projected receipts during January:
                Cash sales during month           xxxx
                Collections from credit sales      xxxx
                      Total cash receipts                     xxxx
         Projected disbursements during January:
                Payments for goods purchased       xxxx
                Salaries                           xxxx
                Rent                               xxxx
                Utilities                          xxxx
                      Total cash disbursements                xxxx
         Cash balance, January 31, 2001                       xxxx
```

1. Open the workbook **Budget** in the Cases folder for Tutorial.01. Save as **BudgetSol**.

2. Enter the following formulas in cells C8, C14, and C15 of your worksheet:

   a. Total cash receipts = Cash receipts during month + Collections from credit sales
   b. Total cash disbursements = Payments for goods purchased + Salaries + Rent + Utilities
   c. Cash Balance, January 31, 2001 = Cash Balance, January 1, 2001 + Total cash receipts – Total cash disbursements

3. Enter the data in Figure 1-31 into the worksheet.

4. Type "Prepared by [your name]" in a cell two rows below the last line of the budget.

Figure 1-31

BUDGET ITEM	AMOUNT	BUDGET ITEM	AMOUNT
Cash balance at beginning of month	32000	Salaries	4800
Cash receipts during month	9000	Rent	1500
Collection from credit sales	17500	Utilities	800
Payments for goods purchased	15000		

5. Save the worksheet.

6. Print the projected cash budget.

7. After printing the budget, Fran remembers that in January the monthly rent increases by $150. Modify the projected cash budget. Print the revised cash budget.

Case 3. *Selecting a Hospital Laboratory Computer System for Bridgeport Medical Center*   David Choi is on the Laboratory Computer Selection Committee for the Bridgeport Medical Center. After an extensive search, the committee has identified three vendors whose products appear to meet its needs. The Selection Committee has prepared an Excel worksheet to help evaluate the strengths and weaknesses of the three potential vendors. The formulas and raw scores for two of the vendors, LabStar and Health Systems, have already been entered. Now the formulas and raw scores must be entered for the third vendor, MedTech. Which vendor's system is best for the Bridgeport Medical Center? Complete these steps to find out which system is best.

1. Open the workbook **Medical** in the Cases folder for Tutorial.01.

2. Use the Save As command to save the workbook as **Medical 2** in the Cases folder for Tutorial 1. That way you won't change the original workbook for this case.

3. Examine the LAB worksheet, and type the following raw scores for MedTech: Cost = 6, Compatibility = 5, Vendor Reliability = 5, Size of Installed Base = 4, User Satisfaction = 5, Critical Functionality = 9, Additional Functionality = 8.

4. Enter the formulas to compute the weighted scores for MedTech in cells E17 to E23. See Figure 1-32.

Figure 1-32

CELL	FORMULA	CELL	FORMULA	CELL	FORMULA
E17	=B6*E6	E20	=B9*E9	E22	=B11*E11
E18	=B7*E7	E21	=B10*E10	E23	=B12*E12
E19	=B8*E8				

5. Enter the formula to compute MedTech's total weighted score.

6. In cell A2 type "Prepared by [your name]".

7. Activate the Documentation worksheet and enter information such as the name of the case, your name, date created, and purposes on this sheet.

8. Use the Save command to save the modified worksheet.

9. Print the worksheet and Documentation sheet.

10. Based on the data in the worksheet, which vendor would you recommend? Why?

11. Assume you can adjust the value for only one importance weight (cells B6 through B12). Which factor would you change and what would its new weight be in order for LabStar to have the highest weighted score? (*Hint*: Remember that the value assigned to any importance weight cannot be higher than 10.)

12. Print the modified worksheet. Close the workbook without saving it.

Case 4. *Cash Counting Calculator*   Rob Stuben works at a local town beach in Narragansett where a fee is collected for parking. At the end of each day, the parking attendants turn in the cash they have collected, with a statement of the daily total. Rob is responsible for receiving the daily cash from each attendant, checking the accuracy of the total, and making the cash deposit to the bank.

Rob wants to set up a simple cash counter using Excel, so that he can insert the number of bills of each denomination into a worksheet and have the total cash automatically computed. By using this method he only has to count and enter the number of one-dollar bills, the number of fives, and so on.

1. Set up this worksheet for Rob. First, list all currency denominations (1, 2, 5, 10, 20, 50, 100) in the first column of your worksheet. The next column will be used to enter the count of the number of bills of each denomination (initially blank). In the third column, enter formulas to calculate totals for each denomination. That is, the number of bills multiplied by the denomination of the bill. Below this total column, enter a formula to calculate the grand total received.

   Next, you want to compare the grand total with the amount reported by an attendant. In the row below the grand total, enter the cash reported by the attendant.

   Finally, below the cash reported amount, enter the formula to calculate the difference between the grand total (calculated amount) and the cash reported by the attendant. The difference should equal zero.

2. On a separate worksheet, create a Documentation sheet. Include the title of the case, your name, date created, and the purpose of the worksheet.

3. On Rob's first day using the worksheet, the cash reported by an attendant was $1,560. Rob counted the bills and entered the following: five 50s, twenty-three 20s, forty-one 10s, sixty-five 5s, and one hundred and twenty 1s. Enter these amounts in your worksheet.

4. Type "Prepared by [your name]" in a cell two rows below the cash calculator worksheet.

5. Save the workbook in the Cases folder of Tutorial.01 using the name **CashCounter**.

6. Print the worksheet.

7. On the second day, the cash reported by an attendant was $1,395. Rob counted the bills and entered the following: two 100s, four 50s, seventeen 20s, thirty-four 10s, forty-five 5s, and ninety 1s. Delete the previous day's count and replace it with the new data.

8. Print the worksheet using the data for the second day.

9. Print the Documentation sheet.

10. Close the workbook without saving changes.

LAB ASSIGNMENTS

The New Perspectives Labs are designed to help you master some of the key computer concepts and skills presented in each chapter of the text. If you are using your school's lab computers, your instructor or technical support person should have installed the Labs software for you. If you want to use the Labs on your home computer, ask your instructor for the appropriate software. See the Read This Before You Begin page for more information on installing and starting the Lab.

Each Lab has two parts: Steps and Explore. Use Steps first to learn and review concepts. Read the information on each page and do the numbered steps. As you work through the Lab, you will be asked to answer Quick Check questions about what you have learned. At the end of the Lab, you will see a Summary Report of your answers to the Quick Checks. If your instructor wants you to turn in this Summary Report, click the Print button on the Summary Report screen.

When you have completed Steps, you can click the Explore button to complete the Lab Assignments. You can also use Explore to practice the skills you learned and to explore concepts on your own.

SPREADSHEETS   Spreadsheet software is used extensively in business, education, science, and humanities to simplify tasks that involve calculations. In this Lab you will learn how spreadsheet software works. You will use spreadsheet software to examine and modify worksheets, as well as to create your own worksheets.

1. Click the Steps button to learn how spreadsheet software works. As you proceed through the Steps, answer all of the Quick Check questions that appear. After you complete the Steps, you will see a Quick Check Summary Report. Follow the instructions on the screen to print this report.

2. Click the Explore button to begin this assignment. Click OK to display a new worksheet. Click File, then click Open to display the Open dialog box. Click the file **Income.xls**, then press the Enter key to open the **Income and Expense Summary** worksheet. Notice that the worksheet contains labels and values for income from consulting and training. It also contains labels and values for expenses such as rent and salaries. The worksheet does not, however, contain formulas to calculate Total Income, Total Expenses, or Profit. Do the following:

   a. Calculate the Total Income by entering the formula =sum(C4:C5) in cell C6.
   b. Calculate the Total Expenses by entering the formula =sum(C9:C12) in C13.
   c. Calculate Profit by entering the formula =C6-C13 in cell C15.
   d. Manually check the results to make sure you entered the formulas correctly.
   e. Print your completed worksheet showing your results.

3. You can use a spreadsheet to keep track of your grade in a class. In Explore, click File, then click Open to display the Open dialog box. Click the file **Grades.xls** to open the Grades worksheet. This worksheet contains the labels and formulas necessary to calculate your grade based on four test scores. You receive a score of 88 out of 100 on the first test. On the second test, you score 42 out of 48. On the third test, you score 92 out of 100. You have not taken the fourth test yet. Enter the appropriate data in the **Grades.xls** worksheet to determine your grade after taking three tests. Print out your worksheet.

4. Worksheets are handy for answering "what if" questions. Suppose you decide to open a lemonade stand. You're interested in how much profit you can make each day. What if you sell 20 cups of lemonade? What if you sell 100? What if the cost of lemons increases?

   In Explore, open the file **Lemons.xls** and use the worksheet to answer questions a through d, then print the worksheet for question e:

   a. What is your profit if you sell 20 cups a day?
   b. What is your profit if you sell 100 cups a day?
   c. What is your profit if the price of lemons increases to $.07 and you sell 100 cups?
   d. What is your profit if you raise the price of a cup of lemonade to $.30? (Lemons still cost $.07 and assume you sell 100 cups.)
   e. Suppose your competitor boasts that she sold 50 cups of lemonade in one day and made exactly $12.00. On your worksheet adjust the cost of cups, water, lemons, and sugar, and the price per cup to show a profit of exactly $12.00 for 50 cups sold. Print this worksheet.

5. It is important to make sure the formulas in your worksheet are accurate. An easy way to test this is to enter 1's for all the values on your worksheet, then check the calculations manually. In Explore, open the worksheet **Receipt.xls**, which calculates sales receipts. Enter 1 as the value for Item 1, Item 2, Item 3, and Sales Tax %. Now, manually calculate what you would pay for three items that cost $1.00 each in a state where sales tax is 1% (.01). Do your manual calculations match those of the worksheet? If not, correct the formulas in the worksheet and print out a *formula report* of your revised worksheet.

6. In Explore, create your own worksheet showing your household budget for one month. You may make up numbers. Put a title on the worksheet. Use formulas to calculate your total income and expenses for the month. Add another formula to calculate how much money you were able to save. Print a formula report of your worksheet. Also, print your worksheet showing realistic values for one month.

INTERNET ASSIGNMENTS

The purpose of the Internet Assignments is to challenge you to find information on the Internet that you can use to create effective documents. The actual assignments are updated and maintained on the Course Technology Web site. Log on to the Internet and use your Web browser to go to the Student Online Companion to accompany this text at **www.course.com/NewPerspectives/office2000**. Click the Excel link, and then click the link for Tutorial 1.

QUICK CHECK ANSWERS

Session 1.1

1. cell

2. open

3. D2

4. b

5. click the "Sheet2" sheet tab

6. press Ctrl + Home

Session 1.2

1. **a.** value **e.** text

   b. text   **f.** text

   c. value **g.** text

   d. formula

2. AutoComplete

3. 7; C3+D3+E3+F3+G3+H3+I3

4. D5,D6,D7,E5,E6,E7,G5,G6,G7

5. When you exit Excel, the workbook is erased from RAM. So if you want to use the workbook again, you need to save it to disk. Click File, then click Save As.

6. revising the contents of one or more cells in a worksheet and observing the effect this change has on all other cells in the worksheet

7. c

8. press the Delete key; click Edit, point to Clear, and then click Contents; click Edit, point to Clear, and then click All.

9. Print, File

OBJECTIVES

In this tutorial you will:

- Plan, build, test, document, preview, and print a worksheet

- Enter labels, values, and formulas

- Calculate a total using the AutoSum button

- Copy formulas using the fill handle and Clipboard

- Learn about relative, absolute, and mixed references

- Use the AVERAGE, MAX, and MIN functions to calculate values in the worksheet

- Spell check the worksheet

- Insert a row

- Reverse an action using the Undo button

- Move a range of cells

- Format the worksheet using AutoFormat

- Center printouts on a page

- Customize worksheet headers

CREATING A WORKSHEET

Producing a Sales Comparison Report for MSI

CASE

Motorcycle Specialties Incorporated

Motorcycle Specialties Incorporated (MSI), a motorcycle helmet and accessories company, provides a wide range of specialty items to motorcycle enthusiasts throughout the world. MSI has its headquarters in Atlanta, Georgia, but it markets products in North America, South America, Australia, and Europe.

The company's marketing and sales director, Sally Caneval, meets regularly with the regional sales managers who oversee global sales in each of the four regions in which MSI does business. This month, Sally intends to review overall sales in each region for the last two fiscal years and present her findings at her next meeting with the regional sales managers. She has asked you to help her put together a report that summarizes this sales information.

Specifically, Sally wants the report to show total sales for each region of the world for the two most recent fiscal years. Additionally, she wants to see the percentage change between the two years. She also wants the report to include the percentage each region contributed to the total sales of the company in 2001. Finally, she wants to include summary statistics on the average, maximum, and minimum sales for 2001.

SESSION 2.1

In this session you will learn how to plan and build a worksheet; enter labels, numbers, and formulas; and copy formulas to other cells.

Developing **Worksheets**

Effective worksheets are well planned and carefully designed. A well-designed worksheet should clearly identify its overall goal. It should present information in a clear, well-organized format and include all the data necessary to produce results that address the goal of the application. The process of developing a good worksheet includes the following planning and execution steps:

- determine the worksheet's purpose, what it will include, and how it will be organized
- enter the data and formulas into the worksheet
- test the worksheet
- edit the worksheet to correct any errors or make modifications
- document the worksheet
- improve the appearance of the worksheet
- save and print the completed worksheet

Planning **the Worksheet**

Sally begins to develop a worksheet that compares global sales by region over two years by creating a planning analysis sheet. Her planning analysis sheet helps her answer the following questions:

1. What is the goal of the worksheet? This helps to define the problem to solve.

2. What are the desired results? This information describes the output—the information required to help solve the problem.

3. What data is needed to calculate the results you want to see? This information is the input—data that must be entered.

4. What calculations are needed to produce the desired output? These calculations specify the formulas used in the worksheet.

Sally's completed planning analysis sheet is shown in Figure 2-1.

Figure 2-1	PLANNING ANALYSIS SHEET

Planning Analysis Sheet

<u>My Goal:</u>
To develop a worksheet to compare annual sales in each region for the last two fiscal years

<u>What results do you want to see?</u>
Sales by region for 2001, 2000
Total Sales for 2001, 2000
Average sales for 2001, 2000
Maximum sales for 2001, 2000
Minimum sales for 2001,2000
Percentage change for each region
Percentage of 2001 sales for each region

<u>What information do I need?</u>
Sales for each region in 2001
Sales for each region in 2000

<u>What calculations do I perform?</u>
Percentage change = (Sales in 2001 − Sales in 2000)/ Sales in 2000
Percentage of 2001 sales = Sales in a region for 2001/Total sales 2001
Total sales for year = Sum of sales for each region
Average sales in 2001
Maximum sales in 2001
Minimum sales in 2001

Next Sally makes a rough sketch of her design, including titles, column headings, row labels, and where data values and totals should be placed. Figure 2-2 shows Sally's sketch. With these two planning tools, Sally is now ready to enter the data into Excel and build the worksheet.

Figure 2-2   SKETCH OF WORKSHEET

Motorcycle Specialties Incorporated
Sales Comparison 2001 with 2000

Region	Year 2001	Year 2000	% Change	% of 2001 Sales
North America	365000	314330	0.16	0.28
South America	354250	292120	0.21	0.28
Australia	251140	262000	-0.04	0.19
Europe	310440	279996	0.11	0.24
Total	1280830	1148446	0.12	

Average   320207.5
Maximum   365000
Minimum   251140

Building the Worksheet

You use Sally's planning analysis sheet, Figure 2-1, and the rough sketch shown in Figure 2-2 to guide you in preparing the sales comparison worksheet. You begin by establishing the layout of the worksheet by entering titles and column headings. Next you work on inputting the data and formulas that will calculate the results Sally needs.

To start Excel and organize your desktop:

1. Start Excel as usual.

2. Make sure your Data Disk is in the appropriate disk drive.

3. Make sure the Microsoft Excel and Book1 windows are maximized.

Entering Labels

When you build a worksheet, it's a good practice to enter the labels before entering any other data. These labels help you identify the cells where you will enter data and formulas in your worksheet. As you type a label in a cell, Excel aligns the label at the left side of the cell. Labels that are too long to fit in a cell spill over into the cell or cells to the right, if those cells are empty. If the cells to the right are not empty, Excel displays only as much of the label as fits in the cell. Begin creating the sales comparison worksheet for Sally by entering the two-line title.

To enter the worksheet title:

1. If necessary, click cell **A1** to make it the active cell.

2. Type **Motorcycle Specialties Incorporated**, and then press the **Enter** key. Since cell A1 is empty, the title appears in cell A1 and spills over into cells B1, C1, and D1. Cell A2 is now the active cell.

TROUBLE? If you make a mistake while typing, remember that you can correct errors with the Backspace key. If you notice the error only after you have pressed the Enter key, then double-click the cell to activate Edit mode, and use the edit keys on your keyboard to correct the error.

3. In cell A2 type **Sales Comparison 2001 with 2000**, and then press the **Enter** key.

Next you enter the column headings defined on the worksheet sketch in Figure 2-2.

To enter labels for the column headings:

1. If necessary, click cell **A3** to make it the active cell.

2. Type **Region** and then press the **Tab** key to complete the entry. Cell B3 is the active cell.

3. Type **Year 2001** in cell B3, and then press the **Tab** key.

   Sally's sketch shows that three more column heads are needed for the worksheet. Enter those next.

4. Enter the remaining column heads as follows:

   Cell C3: **Year 2000**

   Cell D3: **% Change**

   Cell E3: **% of 2001 Sales**

   See Figure 2-3.

   TROUBLE? If any cell does not contain the correct label, either edit the cell or retype the entry.

Figure 2-3	WORKSHEET AFTER TITLES AND COLUMN HEADINGS HAVE BEEN ENTERED

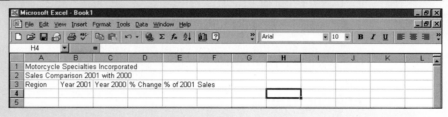

Recall that MSI conducts business in four different regions of the world, and the spreadsheet needs to track the sales information for each region. So Sally wants labels reflecting the regions entered into the worksheet. Enter these labels next.

To enter the regions:

1. Click cell **A4**, type **North America**, and then press the **Enter** key.

2. In cell **A5** type **South America**, and then press the **Enter** key.

3. Type **Australia** in cell A6, and then **Europe** in cell A7.

The last set of labels entered identifies the summary information that will be included in the report.

To enter the summary labels:

1. In cell A8 type **Total**, and then press the **Enter** key.

2. Type the following labels into the specified cells:

   Cell A9: **Average**

   Cell A10: **Maximum**

   Cell A11: **Minimum**

   See Figure 2-4.

Figure 2-4	WORKSHEET AFTER ALL LABELS HAVE BEEN ENTERED

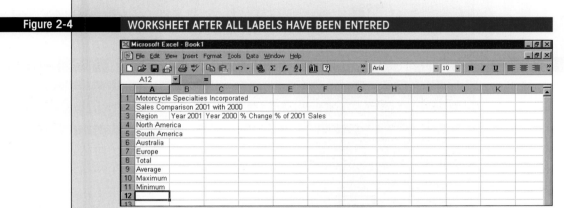

The labels that you just entered into the worksheet will help to identify where the data and formulas need to be placed.

Entering Data

Recall that values can be numbers, formulas, or functions. The next step in building the worksheet is to enter the data, which in this case are the numbers representing sales in each region during 2000 and 2001.

To enter the sales values for 2000 and 2001:

1. Click cell **B4** to make it the active cell. Type **365000** and then press the **Enter** key. See Figure 2-5. Notice that the region name, North America, is no longer completely visible in cell A4 because cell B4 is no longer empty. Later in the tutorial you will learn how to increase the width of a column in order to display the entire contents of cells.

Figure 2-5	WORKSHEET WITH LABEL TRUNCATED IN CELL

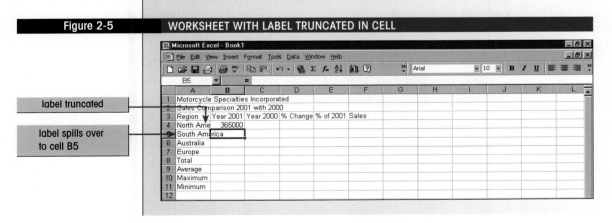

label truncated

label spills over to cell B5

2. In cell B5 type **354250**, and then press the **Enter** key.

3. Enter the values for cells B6, **251140**, and B7, **310440**.

Next, type the values for sales during 2000.

4. Click cell **C4**, type **314330**, and then press the **Enter** key.

5. Enter the remaining values in the specified cells as follows:

Cell C5: **292120**

Cell C6: **262000**

Cell C7: **279996**

Your screen should now look like Figure 2-6.

| Figure 2-6 | WORKSHEET AFTER SALES FOR 2001 AND 2000 HAVE BEEN ENTERED |

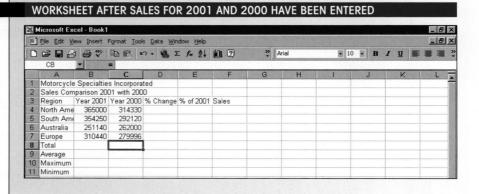

Now that you have entered the labels and data, you need to enter the formulas that will calculate the data to produce the output, or the results. The first calculation Sally wants to see is the total sales for each year. To determine total sales for 2001, you would simply sum the sales from each region for that year. In the previous tutorial you used the SUM function to calculate the weighted total score for the Scottsdale golf site by typing that function into the cell. Similarly, you can use the SUM function to calculate total sales for each year for MSI's comparison report.

Using the AutoSum Button

Since the SUM function is used more often than any other function, Excel includes the AutoSum button on the Standard toolbar. This button automatically creates a formula that contains the SUM function. To do this, Excel looks at the cells adjacent to the active cell, makes an assumption as to which cells you want to sum, and displays a formula based on its best determination about the range you want to sum. You can press the Enter key to accept the formula, or you can select a different range of cells to change the range in the formula. You want to use the AutoSum button to calculate the total sales for each year.

To calculate total sales in 2001 using the AutoSum button:

1. Click cell **B8** because this is where you want to display the total sales for 2001.

2. Click the **AutoSum** button Σ on the Standard toolbar. Excel enters a SUM function in the selected cell and determines that the range of cells to sum is B4:B7, the range directly above the selected cell. See Figure 2-7. In this case, that's exactly what you want to do.

Figure 2-7	USING THE AUTOSUM TOOL

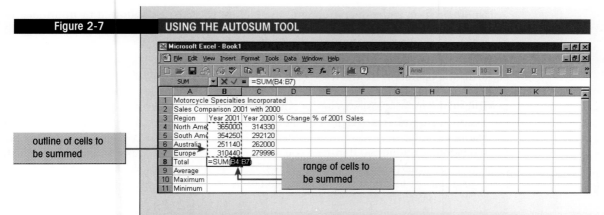

outline of cells to be summed

range of cells to be summed

3. Press the **Enter** key to complete the formula. The result, 1280830, appears in cell B8.

Now use the same approach to calculate the total sales for 2000.

To calculate total sales in 2000 using the AutoSum button:

1. Click cell **C8** to make it the active cell.

2. Click the **AutoSum** Σ button on the Standard toolbar.

3. Press the **Enter** key to complete the formula. The result, 1148446, appears in cell C8.

Next you need to enter the formula to calculate the percentage change in sales for North America between 2001 and 2000.

Entering Formulas

Recall that a formula is an equation that performs calculations in a cell. By entering an equal sign (=) as the first entry in the cell, you are telling Excel that the numbers or symbols that follow constitute a formula, not just data. Reviewing Sally's worksheet plan, you note that you need to calculate the percentage change in sales in North America. The formula is:
Percentage change in sales for North America = (2001 sales in North America - 2000 sales in North America)/2000 sales in North America
So in looking at the worksheet, the formula in Excel would be:
=(B4-C4)/C4
If a formula contains more than one arithmetic operator, Excel performs the calculations in the standard order of precedence of operators, shown in Figure 2-8. The **order of precedence** is a set of predefined rules that Excel uses to unambiguously calculate a formula by determining which part of the formula to calculate first, which part second, and so on.

Figure 2-8	ORDER OF PRECEDENCE FOR ARITHMETIC OPERATIONS

ORDER	OPERATOR	DESCRIPTION
First	^	Exponentiation
Second	* or /	Multiplication or division
Third	+ or -	Addition or subtraction

Exponentiation is the operation with the highest precedence, followed by multiplication and division, and finally addition and subtraction. For example, because multiplication has precedence over addition, the result of the formula =3+4*5 is 23.

When a formula contains more than one operator with the same order of precedence, Excel performs the operation from left to right. Thus, in the formula =4*10/8, Excel multiplies 4 by 10 before dividing the product by 8. The result of the calculation is 5. You can add parentheses to a formula to make it easier to understand or to change the order of operations. Enclosing an expression in parentheses overrides the normal order of precedence. Excel always performs any calculations contained in parentheses first. In the formula =3+4*5, the multiplication is performed before the addition. If instead you wanted the formula to add 3+4 and then multiply the sum by 5, you would enter the formula =(3+4)*5. The result of the calculation is 35. Figure 2-9 shows examples of formulas that will help you understand the order of precedence rules.

Figure 2-9	EXAMPLES ILLUSTRATING ORDER OF PRECEDENCE RULES	
FORMULA VALUE A1=10, B1=20, C1=3	**ORDER OF PRECEDENCE RULE**	**RESULT**
=A1+B1*C1	Multiplication before addition	70
=(A1+B1)*C1	Expression inside parentheses executed before expression outside	90
=A1/B1+C1	Division before addition	3.5
=A1/(B1+C1)	Expression inside parentheses executed before expression outside	.435
=A1/B1*C1	Two operators at same precedence level, leftmost operator evaluated first	1.5
=A1/(B1*C1)	Expression inside parentheses executed before expression outside	.166667

Now enter the percentage change formula as specified in Sally's planning sheet.

To enter the formula for the percentage change in sales for North America:

1. Click cell **D4** to make it the active cell.

2. Type **=(B4-C4)/C4** and then press the **Enter** key. Excel performs the calculations and displays the value 0.1612 in cell D4. The formula is no longer visible in the cell. If you select the cell, the result of the formula appears in the cell, and the formula you entered appears in the formula bar.

Next you need to enter the percentage change formulas for the other regions, as well as the percentage change for the total company sales. You could type the formula =(B5-C5)/C5 in cell D5, the formula =(B6-C6)/C6 in cell D6, the formula =(B7-C7)/C7 in cell D7, and the formula =(B8-C8)/C8 in cell D8. However, this approach is time consuming and error prone. Instead, you can copy the formula you entered in cell C4 (percentage change in North American sales) into cells D5, D6, D7, and D8. Copying duplicates the cell's underlying formula into other cells, automatically adjusting cell references to reflect the new cell address. Copying formulas from one cell to another saves time and reduces the chances of entering incorrect formulas when building worksheets.

Copying a Formula Using the Fill Handle

You can copy formulas using menu commands, toolbar buttons, or the fill handle. The **fill handle** is a small black square located in the lower-right corner of the selected cell, as shown in Figure 2-10. In this section you will use the fill handle to copy the formulas. In other situations you can also use the fill handle for copying values and labels from one cell or a group of cells.

Figure 2-10	FILL HANDLE

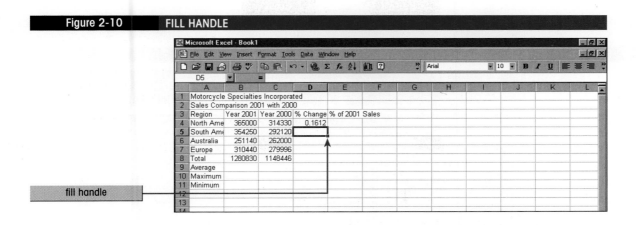

fill handle

Copying Cell Contents with the Fill Handle

- Click the cell that contains the label, value, or formula you want to copy. If you want to copy the contents of more than one cell, select the range of cells you want to copy.
- To copy to adjacent cells, click and drag the fill handle to outline the cells where you want the copy or copies to appear, and then release the mouse button.

You want to copy the formula from cell D4 to cells D5, D6, D7, and D8.

To copy the formula from cell D4 to cells D5, D6, D7, and D8:

1. Click cell **D4** to make it the active cell.

2. Position the pointer over the fill handle (in the lower-right corner of cell D4) until the pointer changes to $+$.

3. Click and drag the pointer down the worksheet to outline cells **D5** through **D8**. See Figure 2-11.

Figure 2-11	COPYING A FORMULA

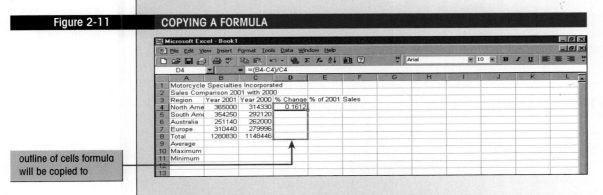

outline of cells formula will be copied to

4. Release the mouse button. Excel copies the formula from D4 to cells D5 to D8. Values now appear in cells D5 through D8.

5. Click any cell to deselect the range. See Figure 2-12.

Figure 2-12   **WORKSHEET AFTER FORMULA HAS BEEN COPIED**

	A	B	C	D	E	F	G	H	I	J	K	L
1	Motorcycle Specialties Incorporated											
2	Sales Comparison 2001 with 2000											
3	Region	Year 2001	Year 2000	% Change	% of 2001 Sales							
4	North Ame	365000	314330	0.1612								
5	South Ame	354250	292120	0.212687								
6	Australia	251140	262000	-0.04145								
7	Europe	310440	279996	0.10873								
8	Total	1280830	1148446	0.115272								
9	Average											
10	Maximum											
11	Minimum											
12												
13												

Notice that Excel didn't copy the formula =(B4-C4)/C4 exactly. It automatically adjusted the cell references for each new formula location. Why did that happen?

Copying a Formula Using Relative References

When you copy a formula that contains cell references, Excel automatically adjusts the cell references for the new locations. For example, when Excel copied the formula from cell D4, =(B4-C4)/C4, it automatically changed the cell references in the formula to reflect the formula's new position in the worksheet. So in cell D5 the cell references adjust to =(B5-C5)/C5. Cell references that change when copied are called **relative cell references**.

Take a moment to look at the formulas in cells D5, D6, D7, and D8.

To examine the formulas in cells D5, D6, D7, and D8:

1. Click cell **D5**. The formula =(B5-C5)/C5 appears in the formula bar.

When Excel copied the formula from cell D4 to cell D5, the cell references changed. The formula =(B4-C4)/C4 became =(B5-C5)/C5 when Excel copied the formula down one row to row 5.

2. Examine the formulas in cells D6, D7, and D8. Notice that the cell references were adjusted for the new locations.

Copying a Formula Using an Absolute Reference

According to Sally's plan, the worksheet should display the percentage that each region contributed to the total sales in 2001. For example, if the company's total sales were $100,000 and sales in North America were $25,000, then sales in North America would be 25% of total sales. To complete this calculation for each region, you need to divide each region's sales by the total company sales, as shown in the following formulas:

Contribution by North America	=B4/B8
Contribution by South America	=B5/B8
Contribution by Australia	=B6/B8
Contribution by Europe	=B7/B8

First enter the formula to calculate the percentage North America contributed to total sales.

To calculate North America's percentage of total 2001 sales:

1. Click cell **E4** to make it the active cell.

2. Type **=B4/B8** and then press the **Enter** key to display the value .284971 in cell E4.

Cell E4 displays the correct result. Sales in North America for 2001 were 365,000, which is approximately .28 of the 1,280,830 in total sales in 2001. Next, you decide to copy the formula in cell E4 to cells E5, E6, and E7.

To copy the percentage formula in cell E4 to cells E5 through E7:

1. Click cell **E4**, and then move the pointer over the fill handle in cell E4 until it changes to $+$.

2. Click and drag the pointer to cell **E7** and release the mouse button.

3. Click any blank cell to deselect the range. The error value "#DIV/0!" appears in cells E5 through E7. See Figure 2-13.

| Figure 2-13 | ERROR VALUE IN WORKSHEET AFTER COPYING FORMULA |

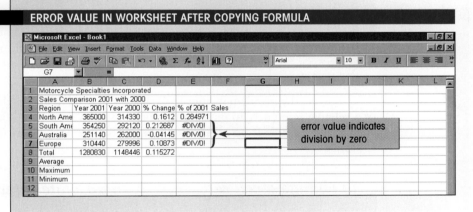

Something is wrong. Cells E5 through E7 display "#DIV/0!" a special constant, called an **error value.** Excel displays an error value constant when it cannot resolve the formula **#DIV/0!**, one of seven error value constants means that Excel was instructed to divide by zero. Take a moment to look at the formulas you copied into cells E5, E6, and E7.

To examine the formulas in cells E5 through E7:

1. Click cell **E5** and then look at the formula appearing in the formula bar, =B5/B9. The first cell reference changed from B4 in the original formula to B5 in the copied formula. That's correct because the sales data for South America is entered in cell B5. The second cell reference changed from B8 in the original formula to B9, which is not correct. The correct formula should be =B5/B8 because the total sales are in cell B8, not cell B9.

2. Look at the formulas in cells E6 and E7 and see how the cell references changed in each formula.

As you observed, the cell reference to total company sales (B8) in the original formula was changed to B9, B10, and B11 in the copied formulas. The problem with the copied formulas is that Excel adjusted *all* the cell references relative to their new location.

Absolute Versus Relative References

Sometimes when you copy a formula, you don't want Excel to change all cell references automatically to reflect their new positions in the worksheet. If you want a cell reference to point to the same location in the worksheet when you copy it, you must use an **absolute reference**. An absolute reference is a cell reference in a formula that does not change when copied to another cell.

To create an absolute reference, you insert a dollar sign ($) before the column and row of the cell reference. For example, the cell reference $B$8 is an absolute reference, whereas the cell reference B8 is a relative reference. If you copy a formula that contains the absolute reference $B$8 to another cell, the cell reference to $B$8 does not change. On the other hand, if you copy a formula containing the relative reference B8 to another cell, the reference to B8 changes. In some situations, a cell might have a **mixed reference**, such as $B8; in this case, when the formula is copied, the row number changes but the column letter does not.

To include an absolute reference in a formula, you can type a dollar sign when you type the cell reference, or you can use the F4 key to change the cell reference type while in Edit mode.

REFERENCE WINDOW   **RW**

Changing Absolute, Mixed, and Relative References
- Double-click the cell that contains the formula you want to edit.
- Use the arrow keys to move the insertion point to the part of the cell reference you want to change.
- Press the F4 key until the reference is correct. Press the Enter key to complete the edit.

To correct the problem in your worksheet, you need to use an absolute reference, instead of a relative reference, to indicate the location of total sales in 2001. That is, you need to change the formula from =B4/B8 to =B4/$B$8. The easiest way to make this change is in Edit mode.

To change a cell reference to an absolute reference:

1. Click cell **E4** to move to the cell that contains the formula you want to edit.

2. Double-click the mouse button to edit the formula in the cell. Notice that each cell reference in the formula in cell E4 appears in a different color and the corresponding cells referred to in the formula are outlined in the same color. This feature is called **Range Finder** and is designed to make it easier for you to check the accuracy of your formula.

3. Make sure the insertion point is to the right of the division (/) operator, anywhere in the cell reference B8.

4. Press the **F4** key to change the reference to $B$8.

   TROUBLE? If your reference shows the **mixed reference** B$8 or $B8, continue to press the F4 key until you see $B$8.

5. Press the **Enter** key to update the formula in cell E4.

Cell E4 still displays .284971, which is the formula's correct result. But remember, the problem in your original formula did not surface until you copied it to cells E5 through E7. To correct the error, you need to copy the revised formula and then check the results. Although you can again use the fill handle to copy the formula, you can also copy the formula using the Clipboard and the Copy and Paste buttons on the Standard toolbar.

Copying Cell Contents Using the Copy-and-Paste Method

You can duplicate the contents of a cell or range by making a copy of the cell or range and then pasting the copy into one or more locations in the same worksheet, another worksheet, or another workbook.

When you copy a cell or range of cells, the copied material is placed on the Clipboard. You can copy labels, numbers, dates, or formulas.

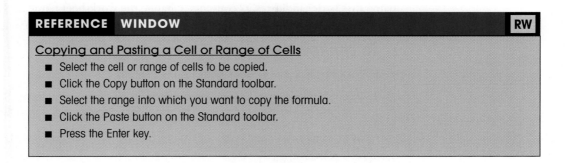

REFERENCE WINDOW   **RW**

Copying and Pasting a Cell or Range of Cells
- Select the cell or range of cells to be copied.
- Click the Copy button on the Standard toolbar.
- Select the range into which you want to copy the formula.
- Click the Paste button on the Standard toolbar.
- Press the Enter key.

You need to copy the formula in cell E4 to the Clipboard and then paste that formula into cells E5 through E7.

To copy the revised formula from cell E4 to cells E5 through E7:

1. Click cell **E4** because it contains the revised formula that you want to copy.

2. Click the **Copy** button 🗐 on the Standard toolbar. A moving dashed line surrounds cell E4, indicating that the formula has been copied and is available to be pasted into other cells.

3. Click and drag to select cells **E5** through **E7**.

4. Click the **Paste** button 🗐 on the Standard toolbar. Excel adjusts the formula and pastes it into cells E5 through E7.

5. Click any cell to deselect the range and view the formulas' results. Press the **Escape** key to clear the Clipboard and remove the dashed line surrounding cell E4. See Figure 2-14.

Figure 2-14   **RESULTS OF COPYING THE FORMULA WITH AN ABSOLUTE REFERENCE**

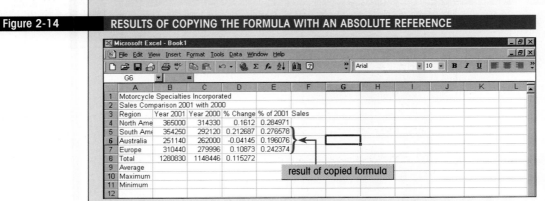

Copying this formula worked. When you pasted the formula from cell E4 into the range E5:E7, Excel automatically adjusted the relative reference (B4), while using the cell reference ($B$8) for all absolute references. You have now implemented most of the design as specified in the planning analysis sheet. Now rename the worksheet to accurately describe its contents, then save the workbook on your Data Disk before entering the formulas to compute the summary statistics.

Renaming the Worksheet

Before saving the workbook, look at the sheet tab in the lower-left corner of the worksheet window: the sheet is currently named Sheet1—the name Excel automatically uses when it opens a new workbook. Now that your worksheet is taking shape, you want to give it a more descriptive name that better indicates its contents. Change the worksheet name to Sales Comparison.

To change a worksheet name:

1. Double-click the **Sheet1** sheet tab to select it.

2. Type the new name, **Sales Comparison**, over the current name, Sheet1, and then click any cell in the worksheet. The sheet tab displays the name "Sales Comparison."

Saving the New Workbook

Now you want to save the workbook. Because this is the first time you have saved this workbook, you use the Save As command and name the file MSI Sales Report.

To save the workbook as MSI Sales Report:

1. Click **File** on the menu bar, and then click **Save As** to open the Save As dialog box.

2. In the File name text box, type **MSI Sales Report** but don't press the Enter key yet. You still need to check some other settings.

3. Click the **Save in** list arrow, and then click the drive containing your Data Disk.

4. In the folder list, select the **Tutorial** folder for **Tutorial.02**, into which you want to save the workbook. Your Save As dialog box should look like the dialog box in Figure 2-15.

Figure 2-15   **SAVING THE WORKBOOK AS MSI SALES REPORT**

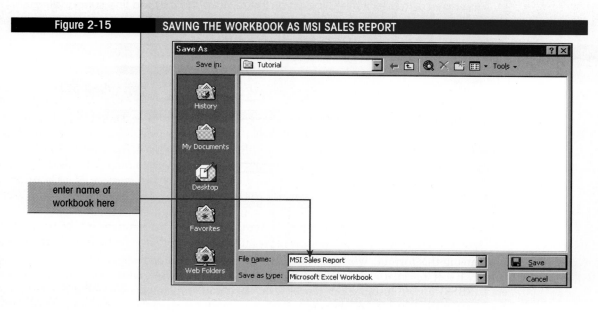

enter name of
workbook here

MAX Function

MAX is a statistical function that finds the largest number. The syntax of the MAX function is: MAX(*number1,number2,...*)

In the MAX function, *number* can be a constant number such as 345, a cell reference such as B6, or a range of cells such as B5:B16. You can use the MAX function to simply display the largest number or to use the largest number in a calculation. Although you can use the Paste Function to enter the MAX function, this time you'll type the MAX function directly into cell B10.

> ### *To enter the MAX function by typing directly into a cell:*
>
> 1. If necessary, click cell **B10** to select it as the cell into which you want to type the formula that uses the MAX function.
>
> 2. Type **=MAX(B4:B7)** and then press the **Enter** key. Cell B10 displays 365000, the largest regional sales amount in 2001.

Next you need to find the smallest regional sales amount in 2001. For that, you'll use the MIN function.

MIN Function

MIN is a statistical function that finds the smallest number. The syntax of the MIN function is: MIN(*number1,number2,...*)

You can use the MIN function to display the smallest number or to use the smallest number in a calculation.

You'll enter the MIN function directly into cell B11 using the pointing method.

Building Formulas by Pointing

Excel provides several ways to enter cell references into a formula. One is to type the cell references directly, as you have done so far in all the formulas you've entered. Another way to put a cell reference in a formula is to point to the cell reference you want to include while creating the formula. To use the **pointing method** to enter the formula, you click the cell or range of cells whose cell references you want to include in the formula. You may prefer to use this method to enter formulas because it minimizes typing errors.

Now use the pointing method to enter the formula to calculate the minimum sales.

> ### *To enter the MIN function using the pointing method:*
>
> 1. If necessary, click cell **B11** to move to the cell where you want to enter the formula that uses the MIN function.
>
> 2. Type **=MIN(** to begin the formula.
>
> 3. Position the cell pointer in cell **B4**, and then click and drag to select cells **B4** through **B7**. As you drag the mouse over the range, notice that the message "4Rx1C" appears in a ScreenTip, informing you that four rows and one column have been selected. See Figure 2-19.

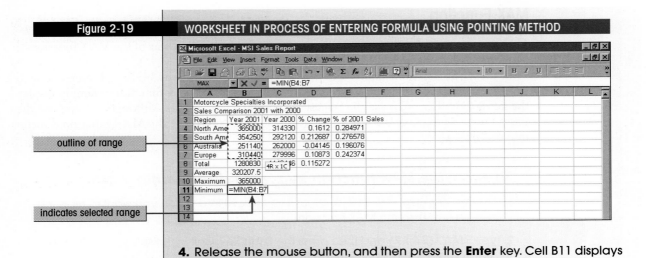

Figure 2-19   WORKSHEET IN PROCESS OF ENTERING FORMULA USING POINTING METHOD

outline of range

indicates selected range

4. Release the mouse button, and then press the **Enter** key. Cell B11 displays
251140, the smallest regional sales amount for 2001.

Now that the worksheet labels, values, formulas, and functions have been entered, Sally
reviews the worksheet.

Testing the Worksheet

Before trusting a worksheet and its results, you should test it to make sure you entered the
correct formulas. You want the worksheet to produce accurate results.

Beginners often expect their Excel worksheets to work correctly the first time. Sometimes
they do work correctly the first time, but even well-planned and well-designed worksheets
can contain errors. It's best to assume that a worksheet has errors and test it to make sure it is
correct. While there are no rules for testing a worksheet, here are some approaches:

- Entering **test values**, numbers that generate a known result, to determine
  whether your worksheet formulas are accurate. For example, try entering a 1
  into each cell. After you enter the test values, you compare the results in
  your worksheet with the known results. If the results on your worksheet
  don't match the known results, you probably made an error.

- Entering **extreme values**, such as very large or very small numbers, and
  observing their effect on cells with formulas.

- Working out the numbers ahead of time with pencil, paper, and calculator,
  and comparing these results with the output from the computer.

Sally used the third approach to test her worksheet. She had calculated her results using a calculator (Figure 2-2) and then compared them with the results on the screen (Figure 2-19). The
numbers agree, so she feels confident that the worksheet she created contains accurate results.

Spell Checking the Worksheet

You can use the Excel spell check feature to help identify and correct spelling and typing
errors. Excel compares the words in your worksheet to the words in its dictionary. If Excel
finds a word in your worksheet not in its dictionary, it shows you the word and some suggested corrections, and you decide whether to correct it or leave it as is.

REFERENCE   WINDOW   **RW**

<u>Checking the Spelling in a Worksheet</u>
- Click cell A1 to begin the spell check from the top of the worksheet.
- Click the Spelling button on the Standard toolbar.
- Change the spelling or ignore the spell check's suggestion for each identified word.
- Click the OK button when the spell check is complete.

You have tested your numbers and formulas for accuracy. Now you can check the spelling of all text entries in the worksheet.

To check the spelling in a worksheet:

1. Click cell **A1** to begin spell checking in the first cell of the worksheet.

2. Click the **Spelling** button on the Standard toolbar to check the spelling of the text in the worksheet. A message box indicates that Excel has finished spell checking the entire worksheet. No errors were found.

   TROUBLE? If the spell check does find a spelling error in your worksheet, use the Spelling dialog box options to correct the spelling mistake and continue checking the worksheet.

Improving the Worksheet Layout

Although the numbers are correct, Sally wants to present a more polished-looking worksheet. She feels that there are a number of simple changes you can make to the worksheet that will improve its layout and make the data more readable. Specifically, she asks you to increase the width of column A so that the entire region names are visible, insert a blank row between the titles and column headings, move the summary statistics down three rows from their current location, and apply one of the predefined Excel formats to the worksheet.

Changing Column Width

Changing the column width is one way to improve the appearance of the worksheet, making it easier to read and interpret data. In Sally's worksheet, you need to increase the width of column A so that all of the labels for North America and South America appear in their cells.

Excel provides several methods for changing column width. For example, you can click a column heading or click and drag the pointer to select a series of column headings and then use the Format menu. You can also use the dividing line between column headings in the column header row. When you move the pointer over the dividing line between two column headings, the pointer changes to ↔. You can then use the pointer to drag the dividing line to a new location. You can also double-click the dividing line to make the column as wide as the longest text label or number in the column.

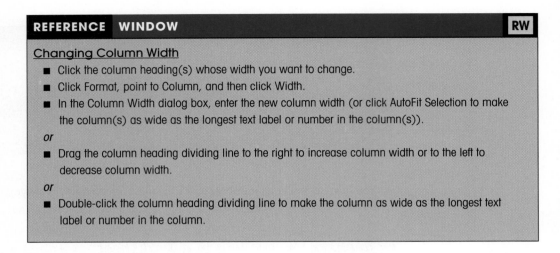

REFERENCE WINDOW   RW

Changing Column Width

- Click the column heading(s) whose width you want to change.
- Click Format, point to Column, and then click Width.
- In the Column Width dialog box, enter the new column width (or click AutoFit Selection to make the column(s) as wide as the longest text label or number in the column(s)).

or

- Drag the column heading dividing line to the right to increase column width or to the left to decrease column width.

or

- Double-click the column heading dividing line to make the column as wide as the longest text label or number in the column.

Sally has asked you to change the width of column A so that the complete region name is visible.

To change the width of column A:

1. Position the pointer ✛ on the A in the column heading area.

2. Move the pointer to the right edge of the column heading dividing columns A and B. Notice that the pointer changes to the resize arrow ↔.

3. Click and drag the resize arrow to the right, increasing the column width 12 characters or more, as indicated in the ScreenTip that pops up on the screen.

4. Release the mouse button. See Figure 2-20.

Figure 2-20   WORKSHEET AFTER WIDTH OF COLUMN A INCREASED

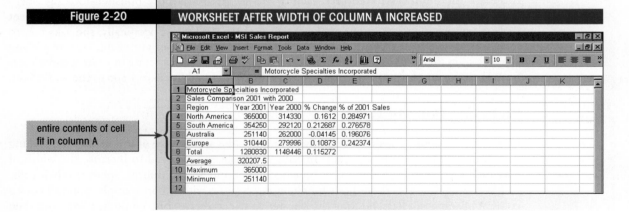

entire contents of cell
fit in column A

Next you need to insert a row between the title and the column heading.

Inserting a Row into a Worksheet

At times you may need to add one or more rows or columns to a worksheet to make room for new data or to make the worksheet easier to read. The process of inserting columns and rows is similar; you select the number of columns or rows you want to insert and then use the Insert command to insert them. When you insert rows or columns, Excel repositions other rows and columns in the worksheet and automatically adjusts cell references in formulas to reflect the new location of values used in calculations.

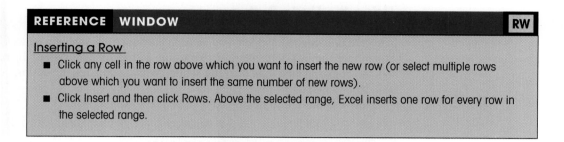

REFERENCE WINDOW   **RW**

Inserting a Row

■ Click any cell in the row above which you want to insert the new row (or select multiple rows above which you want to insert the same number of new rows).

■ Click Insert and then click Rows. Above the selected range, Excel inserts one row for every row in the selected range.

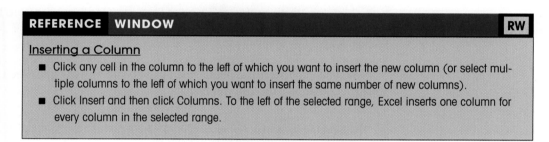

REFERENCE WINDOW   **RW**

Inserting a Column

■ Click any cell in the column to the left of which you want to insert the new column (or select multiple columns to the left of which you want to insert the same number of new columns).

■ Click Insert and then click Columns. To the left of the selected range, Excel inserts one column for every column in the selected range.

Sally wants one blank row between the titles and column headings in her worksheet.

To insert a row into a worksheet:

1. Click cell **A2**.

2. Click **Insert** on the menu bar, and then click **Rows**. Excel inserts a blank row above the original row 2. All other rows shift down one row. Click any cell. See Figure 2-21.

Figure 2-21	WORKSHEET AFTER ONE ROW INSERTED ABOVE ORIGINAL ROW 2

use this button to reverse action

row inserted in wrong position

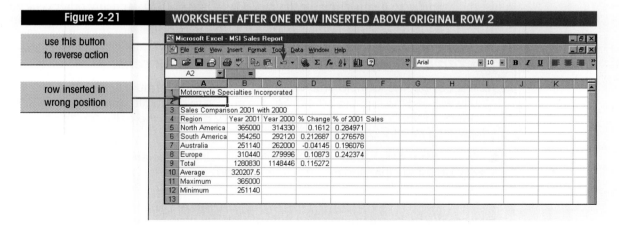

The blank row isn't really where you wanted it. You inserted a row between the two lines of the title instead of between the title and the column heading. To correct this error you can either delete the row or use the Undo button. If you need to delete a row or column, select the row(s) or column(s) you want to delete, then click Delete on the Edit menu, or press the Delete key on your keyboard. You use the Undo button because it is a feature you find valuable in many situations.

Using the Undo Button

The Excel Undo button lets you cancel recent actions one at a time. Click the Undo button to reverse the last command or delete the last entry you typed. To reverse more than one action, click the arrow next to the Undo button and click the action you want to undo from the drop-down list.

Now use the Undo button to reverse the row insertion.

To reverse the row insertion:

1. Click the **Undo** button 🔙 on the Standard toolbar to restore the worksheet to its status before the row was inserted.

Now you can insert the blank row in the correct place—between the second line of the worksheet title and the column heads.

To insert a row into a worksheet:

1. Click cell **A3** because you want to insert one row above row 3. If you wanted to insert several rows, you would select as many rows as you wanted to insert immediately below where you want the new rows inserted before using the Insert command.

2. Click **Insert** on the menu bar, and then click **Rows**. Excel inserts a blank row above the original row 3. All other rows shift down one row.

Adding a row changed the location of the data in the worksheet. For example, the percentage change in North American sales, originally in cell D4, is now in cell D5. Did Excel adjust the formulas to compensate for the new row? Check cell D5 and any other cells you want to view to verify that the cell references were adjusted.

To examine the formula in cell D5 and other cells:

1. Click cell **D5**. The formula =(B5-C5)/C5 appears in the formula bar. You originally entered the formula =(B4-C4)/C4 in cell D4 to calculate percentage change in North America. Excel automatically adjusted the cell reference to reflect the new location of the data.

2. Inspect other cells below row 3 to verify that their cell references were automatically adjusted when the new row was inserted.

Sally has also suggested moving the summary statistics down three rows from their present location to make the report easier to read. So you will need to move the range of cells containing the average, minimum, and maximum sales to a different location in the worksheet.

Moving a Range Using the Mouse

To place the summary statistics three rows below the other data in the report, you could use the Insert command to insert three blank rows between the total and average sales. Alternatively, you could use the mouse to move the summary statistics to a new location. Because you already know how to insert a row, try using the mouse to move the summary statistics to a new location. This technique is called drag and drop. You simply select the cell range you want to move and use the pointer ☝ to drag the cells' contents to the desired location.

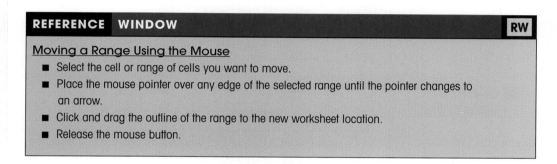

REFERENCE   WINDOW   **RW**

Moving a Range Using the Mouse
- Select the cell or range of cells you want to move.
- Place the mouse pointer over any edge of the selected range until the pointer changes to an arrow.
- Click and drag the outline of the range to the new worksheet location.
- Release the mouse button.

   Sally has asked you to move the range A10 through B12 to the new destination area A13 through B15.

To move a range of cells using the drag-and-drop technique:

1. Select the range of cells **A10:B12,** which contains the sales summary statistics you want to move.

2. Place the mouse pointer over any edge of the selected range until the pointer changes to an arrow ☝. See Figure 2-22.

| Figure 2-22 | RANGE TO BE MOVED |

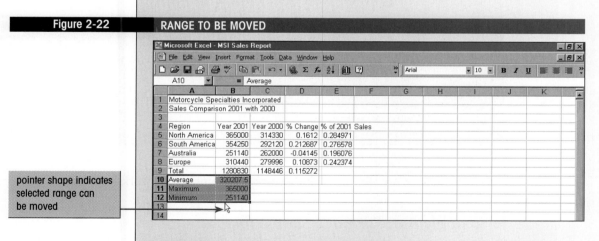

pointer shape indicates selected range can be moved

3. Click the mouse button and then hold the button down as you move (drag) the outline of the three rows down to range A13:B15. Notice how Excel displays a gray outline and a box with a range address that shows the destination of the cells.

4. Release the mouse button. Excel moves the selected cells to the designated location, A13:B15.

5. Click any cell to deselect the range. See Figure 2-23.

Figure 2-23 — WORKSHEET AFTER RANGE MOVED

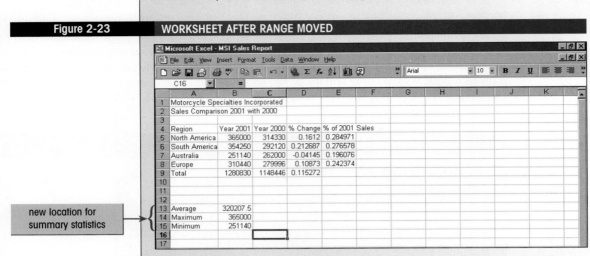

new location for
summary statistics

Next Sally wants you to use the Excel AutoFormat feature to improve the worksheet's appearance by emphasizing the titles and aligning numbers in cells.

Using AutoFormat

The AutoFormat feature lets you change the appearance of your worksheet by selecting from a collection of predefined worksheet formats. Each worksheet format in the AutoFormat collection gives your worksheet a more professional appearance by applying attractive fonts, borders, colors, and shading to a range of data. AutoFormat also adjusts column widths, row heights, and the alignment of text in cells to improve the appearance of the worksheet.

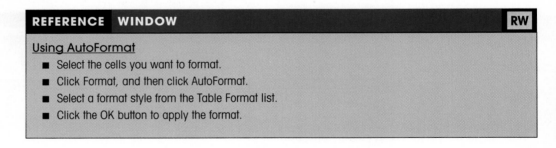

REFERENCE WINDOW | RW

Using AutoFormat
- Select the cells you want to format.
- Click Format, and then click AutoFormat.
- Select a format style from the Table Format list.
- Click the OK button to apply the format.

Now you'll use AutoFormat's Simple format to improve the worksheet's appearance.

To apply AutoFormat's Simple format:

1. Select cells **A1:E9** as the range you want to format using AutoFormat.

2. Click **Format** on the menu bar, and then click **AutoFormat**. The AutoFormat dialog box opens. See Figure 2-24.

Figure 2-24   AUTOFORMAT DIALOG BOX

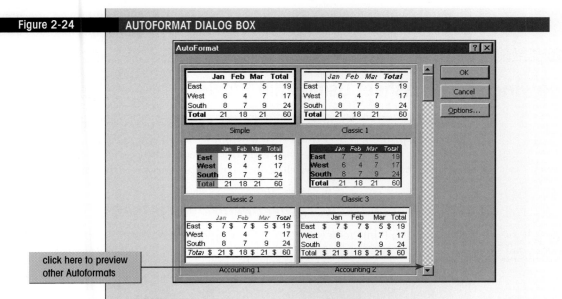

click here to preview other Autoformats

3. The dialog box displays a preview of how each format will appear when applied to a worksheet. Notice the dark border around the Simple format indicating it is the selected format.

4. Click the **OK** button to apply the Simple format.

5. Click any cell to deselect the range. Figure 2-25 shows the newly formatted worksheet.

Figure 2-25   WORKSHEET AFTER USING THE SIMPLE AUTOFORMAT

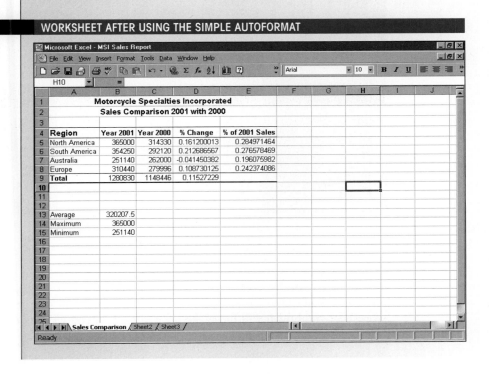

You show the worksheet to Sally. She's impressed with the improved appearance and decides to hand it out to the regional sales managers at their next meeting. She asks you to print it so she can make copies.

Previewing the Worksheet Using Print Preview

Before you print a worksheet, you can use the Excel Print Preview window to see how it will look when printed. The Print Preview window shows you margins, page breaks, headers, and footers that are not always visible on the screen. If the preview isn't what you want, you can close the Print Preview window and change the worksheet before printing it.

To preview the worksheet before you print it:

1. Click the Print Preview button to display the worksheet in the Print Preview window. See Figure 2-26.

   TROUBLE? If you do not see the Print Preview button on the Standard toolbar, click More Buttons to display the Print Preview button.

Figure 2-26   PRINT PREVIEW OF SALES COMPARISON WORKSHEET

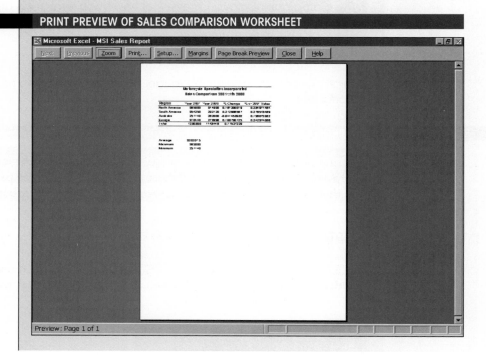

When Excel displays a full page in the Print Preview window, you might have difficulty seeing the text of the worksheet because it is so small. Don't worry if the preview isn't completely readable. One purpose of the Print Preview window is to see the overall layout of the worksheet and how it will fit on the printed page. If you want a better view of the text, you can use the Zoom button.

To display an enlarged section of the Print Preview window:

1. Click the **Zoom** button to display an enlarged section of the Print Preview.

2. Click the **Zoom** button again to return to the full-page view.

Notice that the Print Preview window contains several other buttons. Figure 2-27 describes each of these buttons.

Figure 2-27	DESCRIPTION OF PRINT PREVIEW BUTTONS
CLICKING THIS BUTTON	**RESULTS IN**
Next	Moving forward one page
Previous	Moving backward one page
Zoom	Magnifying the Print Preview screen to zoom in on any portion of the page; click again to return to full-page preview
Print	Printing the document
Setup	Displaying the Page Setup dialog box
Margins	Changing the width of margins, columns in the worksheet and the position of headers and footers
Page Break Preview	Showing where page breaks occur in the worksheet and which area of the worksheet will be printed; you can adjust where data will print by inserting or moving page breaks
Close	Closing the Print Preview window
Help	Activating Help

Looking at the worksheet in Print Preview, you observe that it is not centered on the page. By default, Excel prints a worksheet at the upper left of the page's print area. You can specify that the worksheet be centered vertically, horizontally, or both.

Centering the Printout

Worksheet printouts generally look more professional centered on the printed page. You decide that Sally would want you to center the sales comparison worksheet both horizontally and vertically on the printed page.

To center the printout:

1. In Print Preview, click the **Setup** button to open the Page Setup dialog box.

2. Click the **Margins** tab. See Figure 2-28. Notice that the preview box displays a worksheet positioned at the upper-left edge of the page.

Figure 2-28   MARGINS TAB OF PAGE SETUP DIALOG BOX

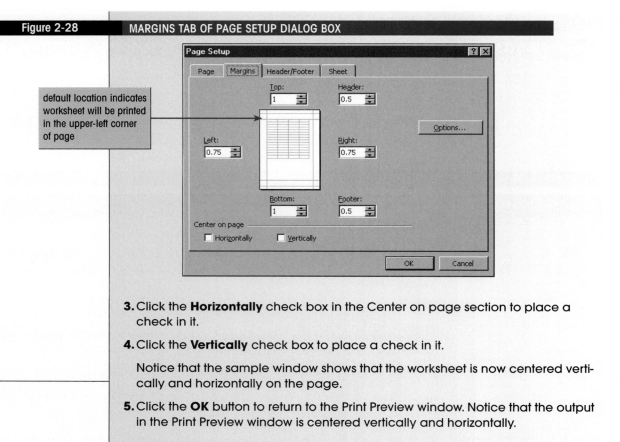

default location indicates worksheet will be printed in the upper-left corner of page

3. Click the **Horizontally** check box in the Center on page section to place a check in it.

4. Click the **Vertically** check box to place a check in it.

   Notice that the sample window shows that the worksheet is now centered vertically and horizontally on the page.

5. Click the **OK** button to return to the Print Preview window. Notice that the output in the Print Preview window is centered vertically and horizontally.

   TROUBLE? If you see only the worksheet name, click the Zoom button to view the entire page.

Adding Headers and Footers

Headers and footers can provide useful documentation on your printed worksheet, such as the name of the person who created the worksheet, the date it was printed, and its filename. The **header** is text printed in the top margin of every worksheet page. A **footer** is text printed in the bottom margin of every page. Headers and footers are not displayed in the worksheet window. To see them, you must preview or print the worksheet.

Excel uses formatting codes in headers and footers to represent the items you want to print. Formatting codes produce dates, times, and filenames that you might want a header or footer to include. Using formatting codes instead of typing the date, time, filename and so on provides flexibility. For example, if you use a formatting code for date, the current date appears on the printout whenever the worksheet is printed. You can type these codes, or you can click a formatting code button to insert the code. Figure 2-29 shows the formatting codes and the buttons for inserting them.

Figure 2-29		HEADER AND FOOTER FORMATTING BUTTONS	
BUTTON	**BUTTON NAME**	**FORMATTING CODE**	**ACTION**
A	Font	none	Sets font, text style, and font size
#	Page number	&[Page]	Inserts page number
⊞	Total pages	&[Pages]	Inserts total number of pages
🗓	Date	&[Date]	Inserts current date
🕐	Time	&[Time]	Inserts current time
🗎	Filename	&[File]	Inserts filename
🖥	Sheet name	&[Tab]	Inserts name of active worksheet

Sally asks you to add a custom header that includes the filename and today's date. She also wants you to add a custom footer that displays the preparer's name.

To add a header and a footer to your worksheet:

1. In the Print Preview window, click the **Setup** button to open the Page Setup dialog box, and then click the **Header/Footer** tab.

2. Click the **Custom Header** button to open the Header dialog box.

3. With the insertion point in the Left section box, click the **Filename** button 🗎 . The code &(File) appears in the Left section box.

   TROUBLE? If you clicked the wrong code, double-click the code, press the Delete key, then repeat Steps 2 and 3.

4. Click the **Right section** box to move the insertion point to the Right section box.

5. Click the **Date** button 🗓 . The code &(Date) appears in the Right section box. See Figure 2-30.

Figure 2-30	INSERTING FORMATTING CODES INTO THE HEADER DIALOG BOX

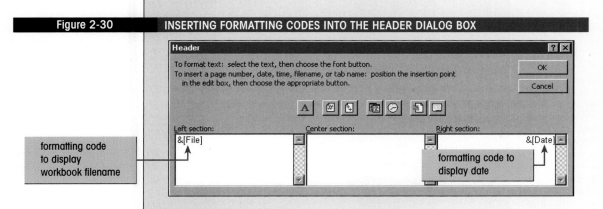

formatting code to display workbook filename

formatting code to display date

TROUBLE? If you clicked the wrong code, double-click the code, press the Delete key, and then repeat Step 5.

6. Click the **OK** button to complete the header and return to the Page Setup dialog box. Notice that the header shows the filename on the left and the date on the right.

7. Click the **Custom Footer** button to open the Footer dialog box.

8. Click the **Center section** box to move the insertion point to the Center section box.

9. Type **Prepared by (*enter your name here*).**

10. Click the **OK** button to complete the footer and return to the Page Setup dialog box. Notice that the footer shows your name in the bottom, center of the page.

11. Click the **OK** button to return to the Print Preview window. The new header and footer appear in the Print Preview window.

12. Click the **Close** button to exit the Print Preview window and return to the worksheet.

You'll use the Print button on the Standard toolbar to print one copy of the worksheet with the current settings. First, save the worksheet before printing it.

To save your page setup settings with the worksheet and print the worksheet:

1. Click the **Save** button 🖫 on the Standard toolbar.

2. Click the **Print** button 🖨 on the Standard toolbar. See Figure 2-31.

   TROUBLE? If you see a message that indicates that you have a printer problem, click the Cancel button to cancel printing. Check your printer to make sure it is turned on and is online; also make sure it has paper. Then go back and try Step 2 again. If you have no printer available, click the Cancel button.

| Figure 2-31 | PRINTED WORKSHEET |

Motorcycle Specialties Incorporated
Sales Comparison 2001 with 2000

Region	Year 2001	Year 2000	% Change	% of 2001 Sales
North America	365000	314330	0.161200013	0.284971464
South America	354250	292120	0.212686567	0.276578469
Australia	251140	262000	-0.041450382	0.196075982
Europe	310440	279996	0.108730125	0.242374086
Total	1280830	1148446	0.11527229	

Average	320207.5
Maximum	365000
Minimum	251140

Sally reviews the printed worksheet and is satisfied with its appearance. Now she asks for a second printout without the average, minimum, and maximum statistics.

Setting the Print Area

By default, Excel prints the entire worksheet. There are situations in which you are interested in printing a portion of the worksheet. To do this, you first select the area you want to print, and then use the Set Print Area command to define the print area.

> ## To print a portion of the worksheet:
>
> 1. Select the range **A1:E9**.
>
> 2. Click **File**, point to Print Area, and then click **Set Print Area**.
>
> 3. Click the **Print Preview** button. Notice the average, minimum and maximum values are not included in the print preview window.
>
> 4. Click **Close** to return to the worksheet.
>
> 5. Click any cell outside the highlighted range. Notice the range A1: E9 is surrounded with a dashed line indicating the current print area for the worksheet.

If you want to print the entire worksheet once a print area has been set, you need to remove the current print area. Select File, point to Print Area, and click the Clear Print Area to remove the print area. Now the entire worksheet will print.

Documenting the Workbook

Documenting the workbook provides valuable information to those using the workbook. Documentation includes external documentation as well as notes and instructions within the workbook. This information could be as basic as who created the worksheet and the date it was created, or it could be more detailed, including formulas, summaries, and layout information.

Depending on the use of the workbook, the required amount of documentation varies. Sally's planning analysis sheet and sketch for the sales comparison worksheet are one form of external documentation. This information can be useful to someone who would need to modify the worksheet in any way because it states the goals, required input, output, and the calculations used.

One source of internal documentation would be a worksheet placed as the first worksheet in the workbook, such as the Documentation worksheet in Tutorial 1 to determine the best location for the new Inwood golf course. In more complex workbooks, this sheet may also include an index of all worksheets in the workbook, instructions on how to use the worksheets, where to enter data, how to save the workbook, and how to print reports. This documentation method is useful because the information is contained directly in the workbook and can easily be viewed upon opening the workbook, or printed if necessary. Another source of internal documentation is the **Property** dialog box. This dialog box enables you to electronically capture information such as the name of the workbook's creator, the creation date, the number of revisions, and other information related to the workbook.

If you prefer, you can include documentation on each sheet of the workbook. One way is to attach notes to cells by using the Comments command to explain complex formulas, list assumptions, and enter reminders.

The worksheet itself can be used as documentation. Once a worksheet is completed, it is a good practice to print and file a hardcopy of your work as documentation. This hardcopy file should include a printout of each worksheet displaying the values and another printout of the worksheet displaying the cell formulas.

Sally asks you to include a note in the worksheet that will remind her that the sales in Europe do not include an acquisition that was approved in December. You suggest inserting a cell comment.

Adding Cell Comments

Cell comments can help users remember assumptions, explain complex formulas, or place reminders related to the contents of a specific cell.

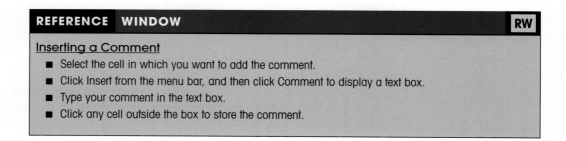

REFERENCE WINDOW   **RW**

Inserting a Comment
- Select the cell in which you want to add the comment.
- Click Insert from the menu bar, and then click Comment to display a text box.
- Type your comment in the text box.
- Click any cell outside the box to store the comment.

Use the cell comment to insert the note for Sally.

To add a comment to a cell:

1. Click cell **B8**.

2. Click **Insert** and then click **Comment** to display a text box.

   TROUBLE? If the Comment item does not appear on the Insert menu, click ⚡ to view additional items on the Insert menu.

   Now enter your comment in the text box.

3. Type **Does not include sales from company acquired in December**. See Figure 2-32.

Figure 2-32   INSERTING A CELL COMMENT

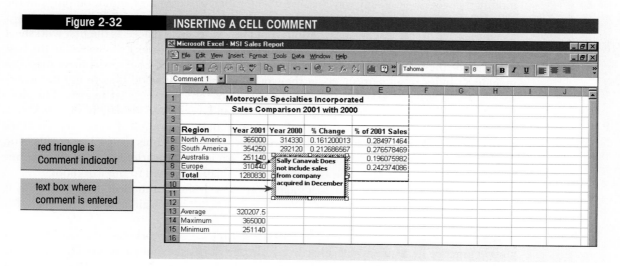

4. Click any cell outside the text box. The comment disappears. Notice, the **Comment indicator**, a tiny red triangle, appears in the upper-right corner of the cell indicating the cell contains a comment.

Now view the comment.

TROUBLE? If the comment remains on the screen, click View, then click Comments.

5. Move the mouse pointer over cell **B8**. The Comment appears, preceded by the name of the user who made the comment.

6. Move the mouse pointer to another cell. The comment disappears.

7. Save the workbook.

Once a comment is inserted, you can edit or delete the comment by right-clicking the cell and selecting Edit Comment or Delete Comment from the shortcut menu.

Now Sally asks for a printout of the worksheet formulas for her file.

Displaying and Printing Worksheet Formulas

You can document the formulas you entered in a worksheet by displaying and printing them. When you display formulas, Excel shows the formulas you entered in each cell instead of showing the results of the calculations. You want a printout of the formulas in your worksheet for documentation.

To display worksheet formulas:

1. Click **Tools** on the menu bar, and then click **Options** to open the Options dialog box.

2. Click the **View** tab, and then click the **Formulas** check box in the Window options section to select it.

3. Click the **OK** button to return to the worksheet. The width of each column nearly doubles to accommodate the underlying formulas. See Figure 2-33.

| Figure 2-33 | DISPLAYING FORMULAS IN A WORKSHEET |

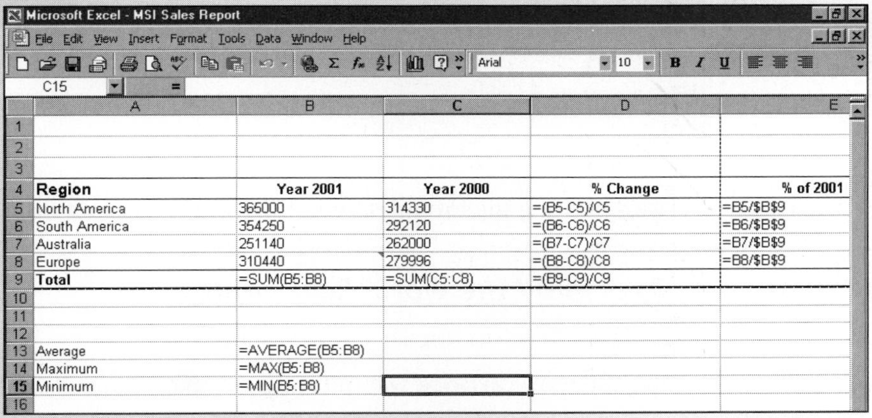

You may find the keyboard shortcut, Ctrl + ` (` is found next to the 1 in the upper-left area of the keyboard) easier to use when displaying formulas. Press the shortcut key once to display formulas and again to display results.

Now print the worksheet displaying the formulas. Before printing the formulas, you need to change the appropriate settings in the Page Setup dialog box to show the gridlines and the row/column headings, center the worksheet on the page, and fit the printout on a single page.

To adjust the print setups to display formulas:

1. Click **File** on the menu bar, and then click **Page Setup** to open the Page Setup dialog box.

2. Click the **Sheet** tab to view the sheet options, and then click the **Row and Column Headings** check box in the Print section to print the row numbers and column letters along with the worksheet results.

3. Click the **Gridlines** check box to select that option.

4. Click the **Page** tab and then click the **Landscape** option button. This option prints the worksheet with the paper positioned so it is wider than it is tall.

5. Click the **Fit to** option button in the Scaling section of the Page tab. This option reduces the worksheet when you print it, so it fits on the specific number of pages in the Fit to check box. The default is 1.

6. Click the **Print Preview** button to open the Print Preview window.

7. Click the **Print** button. See Figure 2-34. Notice that your printout does not include the formulas for average, minimum and maximum because the print area is still set for the range A1:E9.

| Figure 2-34 | PRINTOUT OF WORKSHEET FORMULAS |

row and column heading printed with formulas

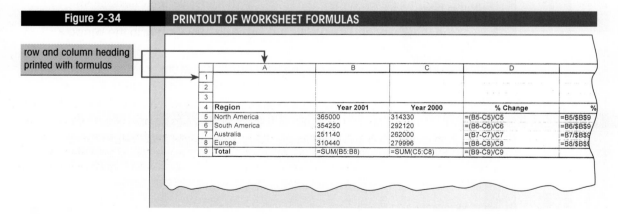

	A	B	C	D	
1					
2					
3					
4	Region	Year 2001	Year 2000	% Change	%
5	North America	365000	314330	=(B5-C5)/C5	=B5/$B$9
6	South America	354250	292120	=(B6-C6)/C6	=B6/$B$9
7	Australia	251140	262000	=(B7-C7)/C7	=B7/$B$9
8	Europe	310440	279996	=(B8-C8)/C8	=B8/$B$9
9	Total	=SUM(B5:B8)	=SUM(C5:C8)	=(B9-C9)/C9	

After printing the formulas, return the worksheet so it displays the worksheet values.

To display the worksheet values:

1. Press **Ctrl + `** to display the worksheet values.

2. Close the workbook without saving it, and then exit Excel.

Session 2.2 QUICK CHECK

1. What is meant by syntax?

2. In the function MAX(A1:A8), identify the function name. Identify the argument(s).

3. Describe how you use the pointing method to create a formula that includes the SUM function.

4. Describe how to insert a row or a column.

5. To reverse your most recent action, which button should you click?

   a. ▣
   b. ▣
   c. ↰

6. To move a range of cells, you must _____ the range first.

7. _____ is a command that lets you change your worksheet's appearance by selecting a collection of predefined worksheet formats.

8. A _____ is text that is printed in the top margin of every worksheet page.

9. A _____ is a tiny red triangle in the upper-right corner of a cell that indicates the cell contains a _____ .

10. To display formulas instead of values in your worksheet, what command should you choose?

11. If your worksheet has too many columns to fit on one printed page, you should try _____ orientation.

You have planned, built, formatted, and documented Sally's sales comparison worksheet. It is ready for her to present to the regional sales managers at their next meeting.

REVIEW ASSIGNMENTS

After Sally meets with the regional sales managers for MSI, she decides it would be a good idea to provide the managers with their own copy of the sales comparison worksheet, so they can update the report with next year's sales data and also modify it to use for their own sales tracking purposes. Before passing it on to them, she wants to provide more documentation and add some additional information that the managers thought would be useful to them. Complete the following for Sally:

1. Start Windows and Excel, if necessary. Insert your Data Disk into the appropriate disk drive. Make sure the Excel and Book1 windows are maximized.

2. Open the workbook **MSI 1** in the Review folder for Tutorial 2 on your Data Disk.

3. Save your workbook as **MSI Sales Report 2** in the Review folder for Tutorial 2 on your Data Disk.

4. Make Sheet2 the active sheet. Use Sheet2 to include information about the workbook. Insert the information in Figure 2-35 into Sheet2. Increase the width of column A as necessary.

Figure 2-35

CELL	TEXT ENTRY
A1	Motorcycle Specialties Incorporated
A3	Created by:
A4	Date Created:
A6	Purpose:
B3	enter your name
B4	enter today's date
B6	Sales report comparing sales by region 2001 with 2000

5. Change the name of the worksheet from **Sheet2** to **Documentation** and print the Documentation sheet.

Explore

6. Move the Documentation sheet so it is the first sheet in the workbook.

7. Make Sales Comparison the active sheet.

8. Insert a row between Australia and Europe. Add the following data (Africa, 125000, 100000) in columns A, B, and C. Copy the formulas for % Change and % of 2001 Sales into the row containing the data for Africa.

9. Open the Office Assistant and then enter the search phrase "Insert a column" to obtain instructions on inserting a new column into a worksheet. Insert a new column between columns C and D.

10. In cell D4, enter the heading "Change".

11. In cell D5, enter the formula to calculate the change in sales for North America from 2000 to 2001. (*Hint*: Check that the figure in cell D5 is 50670.)

12. Copy the formula in D5 to the other regions and total (D6 through D10) using the fill handle.

13. Calculate summary statistics for the year 2000. In cell C14 display the average sales, in cell C15 display the maximum, and in cell C16 display the minimum.

14. Save the workbook.

15. Print the sales comparison worksheet.

16. a. Insert the following comment into cell F4: "Divide 2001 sales in each region by total sales in 2001".
    b. Use the Office Assistant to learn how to print comments to a cell. List the steps.

17. a. Insert a new sheet into the workbook using the Worksheet command from the Insert menu. Activate the **Sales Comparison** sheet and select the range A1:E10. Copy the selected range to the Clipboard. Activate Sheet1 and paste the selected range to the corresponding cells in Sheet1. Apply a different AutoFormat to this range. Print Sheet1. *Note:* If the Office Clipboard toolbar appears, you can use the Office Assistant to learn "About collecting and pasting multiple items" in the Office Clipboard.
    b. Use the Delete Sheet command from the Edit menu to delete Sheet1.
    c. Save the workbook.

CASE PROBLEMS

Case 1. Annual Stockholders' Meeting at MJ Inc.   Jeanne Phelp, chief financial officer (CFO) of MJ Incorporated is responsible for preparing the annual financial reports and mailing them to stockholders before the annual stockholder's meeting. She has completed some of the work for the annual meeting and is now in the process of finishing a report comparing the changes in net income between the current year and last year. Now you can help her complete this report.

1. Use columns A through D to enter the title, labels, and constants from Figure 2-36 into a worksheet.

Figure 2-36   **MJ INCORPORATED INCOME STATEMENT**

	2001	2000	PERCENTAGE CHANGE
Net Sales	1818500	1750500	
Cost of Goods Sold	1005500	996000	
Gross Profit			
Selling and Administrative expenses	506000	479000	
Income from Operations			
Interest expense	18000	19000	
Income before taxes			
Income tax expense	86700	77000	
Net Income			
Outstanding shares	20000	20000	
Earnings Per Share			

2. Complete the income statement for 2001 and 2000 by entering the following formulas for each year:

   ■ Gross profit = Net sales – Cost of goods sold
   ■ Income from operations = Gross profit – Selling and administrative expenses
   ■ Income before taxes = Income from operations – Interest expense
   ■ Net income = Income before taxes – Income tax expense

3. Compute the percentage change between the two years for each item in the income statement.

4. Compute earnings per share (net income / outstanding shares).

5. In cell B4 add the cell comment "Unaudited results".

6. Select an AutoFormat to improve the appearance of your worksheet.

7. Prepare a Documentation sheet, and then place it as the first sheet in the workbook.

8. Save the workbook as **MJ Income** in the Cases folder for Tutorial 2 on your Data Disk. *Note:* The workbook should open so the user can see the contents of the Documentation sheet. (*Hint:* Make the Documentation sheet the active sheet before you save the workbook.)

9. Add your name and date in the custom footer, then print the worksheet, centered horizontally and vertically.

10. Print the Documentation sheet.

11. Save the worksheet, and then print the formulas for the worksheet. Include row and column headings in the output. Do not save the workbook after printing the formulas.

Case 2. Compiling Data on the U.S. Airline Industry　　The editor of *Aviation Week and Space Technology* has asked you to research the current status of the U.S. airline industry. You collect information on the revenue-miles and passenger-miles for each major U.S. airline (Figure 2-37).

Figure 2-37	REVENUE-MILES AND PASSENGER MILES FOR MAJOR U.S. AIRLINES	

AIRLINE	REVENUE-MILES (IN 1000S OF MILES)	PASSENGER-MILES (IN 1000S OF MILES)
American	26000	2210000
Continental	9300	620500
Delta	21500	1860000
Northwest	20800	1900500
US Airways	9850	1540000
United	35175	3675000

You want to calculate the following summary information to use in the article:

- total revenue-miles for the U.S. airline industry
- total passenger-miles for the U.S. airline industry
- each airline's share of the total revenue-miles
- each airline's share of the total passenger-miles
- average revenue-miles for U.S. airlines
- average passenger-miles for U.S. airlines

In order to provide the editor with your researched information, complete these steps:

1. Open a new workbook and then enter the title, column and row labels, and data from Figure 2-37.

2. Enter the formulas to compute the total and average revenue-miles and passenger-miles. Use the SUM and AVERAGE functions where appropriate. Remember to include row labels to describe each statistic.

3. Add a column to display each airline's share of the total revenue-miles. Remember to include a column heading. You decide the appropriate location for this data.

4. Add a column to display each airline's share of the total passenger-miles. Remember to include a column heading. You decide the appropriate location for this data.

5. In a cell two rows after the row of data you entered, insert a line reading : "Compiled by: *XXXX*", where *XXXX* is your name.

6. Rename the worksheet tab Mileage Data.

7. Save the worksheet as **Airline** in the Cases folder for Tutorial 2.

8. Print the worksheet. Make sure you center the report, do not include gridlines, and place the date in the upper-right corner of the header.

9. Select an AutoFormat to improve the appearance of your output.

10. Save your workbook.

11. Print the worksheet, centered on the page.

12. Save the worksheet and then print the formulas for the worksheet. Include row and column headings in the printout.

Case 3. Fresh Air Sales Incentive Program   Carl Stambaugh is assistant sales manager at Fresh Air Inc., a manufacturer of outdoors and expedition clothing. Fresh Air sales representatives contact retail chains and individual retail outlets to sell the Fresh Air line.

This year, to stimulate sales, Carl has decided to run a sales incentive program for sales representatives. Each sales representative has been assigned a sales goal 12% higher than his or her total sales last year. All sales representatives who reach this new goal will be awarded an all-expenses-paid trip for two to Cozumel, Mexico.

Carl wants to track the results of the sales incentive program with an Excel worksheet. He has asked you to complete the worksheet by adding the formulas to compute:

- actual sales in 2001 for each sales representative
- sales goal in 2001 for each sales representative
- percentage of goal reached for each sales representative

He also wants a printout before he presents the worksheet at the next sales meeting. Complete these steps:

1. Open the workbook **Fresh** in the Cases folder for Tutorial 2 on your Data Disk. Maximize the worksheet window and then save the workbook as **Fresh Air Sales Incentives** in the Cases folder for Tutorial 2.

2. Complete the worksheet by adding the following formulas:
    a. 2001 actual for each employee = Sum of actual sales for each quarter
    b. Goal 2001 for each employee = 2000 Sales X (1 + Goal % increase)
    c. % goal reached for each employee = 2001 actual / 2001 goal

    (*Hint:* Use the Copy command. Review relative versus absolute references.)

3. At the bottom of the worksheet (three rows after the last sales rep), add the average, maximum, and minimum statistics for columns C through I.

4. Make formatting changes using an Autoformat to improve the appearance of the worksheet. Begin the formatting in row 6.

5. In cell C4, insert the cell comment "entered sales goal values between 10 and 15 percent".

6. Save the workbook.

7. Print the worksheet. Make sure you center the worksheet horizontally, add an appropriate header, and place your name, course, and date in the footer. Print the worksheet so it fits on one page.

8. Add a Documentation sheet. Save the workbook and then print the Documentation worksheet.

9. Change the sales goal to 14 percent. Print the worksheet.

Explore   10. As you scroll down the worksheet, the column headings no longer appear on the screen, making it difficult to know what each column represents. Use the Office Assistant to look up "Keep column labels visible." Implement this feature in your worksheet. Save the workbook. Explain the steps you take to keep the columns visible.

11. Print the formulas in columns H, I, and J. The printout should include row and column headings. Use the Set Print Area command so you only print the formulas in these three columns. Do not save the workbook after you complete this step.

Case 4. Stock Portfolio for Juan Cortez   Your close friend, Juan Cortez, works as an accountant at a local manufacturing company. While in college, with a double major in accounting and finance, Juan dabbled in the stock market and expressed an interest in becoming a financial planner and running his own firm. To that end, he has continued his professional studies in the evenings with the aim of becoming a certified financial planner. He has already begun to provide financial planning services to a few clients. Because of his hectic schedule as a full-time accountant, part-time student, and part-time financial planner, Juan finds it difficult to keep up with the data-processing needs for his clients. You have offered to assist him.

Juan asks you to set up a worksheet to keep track of a stock portfolio for one of his clients.

Open a new workbook and do the following:

1. Figure 2-38 shows the data you will enter into the workbook. For each stock, you will enter the name, number of shares purchased, and purchase price. Periodically, you will also enter the current price of each stock so Juan can review the changes with his clients.

Figure 2-38

STOCK	NO. OF SHARES	PURCHASE PRICE	COST	CURRENT PRICE	CURRENT VALUE	GAINS/LOSSES
Excite	100	67.30		55.50		
Yahoo	250	121		90.625		
Netscape	50	24.50		26.375		
Microsoft	100	89.875		105.375		
Intel	50	69		83		

2. In addition to entering the data, you need to make the following calculations:
   a. Cost = No. of shares * Purchase price
   b. Current value = No. of shares * Current price
   c. Gains/Losses = Current value minus cost
   d. Totals for cost, Current value, and Gains/Losses

Enter the formulas to calculate the cost, current value, gains/losses, and totals.

3. In the cell where you enter the label for Current Price, insert the cell comment "As of 9/1/2001".

4. Apply an AutoFormat that improves the appearance of the worksheet.

5. Add a Documentation sheet to the workbook.

6. Save the workbook as **Portfolio** in the Cases folder for Tutorial 2.

7. Print the worksheet. Make sure you center the worksheet horizontally and add an appropriate header and footer.

8. Print the Documentation sheet.

9. Clear the prices in the Current Price column of the worksheet.

10. Enter the following prices:

Excite	57.250
Yahoo	86.625
Netscape	30.75
Microsoft	102.375
Intel	84.375

Print the worksheet.

11. Print the formulas for the worksheet. Make sure you include row and column headings in the printed output.

12. From the financial section of your newspaper, look up the current price of each stock (all these stocks are listed on the NASDAQ Stock Exchange). Enter these prices in the worksheet. Print the worksheet.

INTERNET ASSIGNMENTS

The purpose of the Internet Assignments is to challenge you to find information on the Internet that you can use to create effective documents. The actual assignments are updated and maintained on the Course Technology Web site. Log on to the Internet and use your Web browser and go to the Student Online Companion to accompany this text at **www.course.com/NewPerspectives/office2000**. Click the Excel link, and then click the link for Tutorial 2.

QUICK CHECK ANSWERS

Session 2.1

1. Determine the purpose of the worksheet, enter the data and formulas, test the worksheet; correct errors, improve the appearance, document the worksheet, save and print.

2. Select the cell where you want the sum to appear. Click the AutoSum button. Excel suggests a formula that includes the SUM function. To accept the formula press the Enter key.

3. =B4-C4

4. fill handle

5. Cell references; if you were to copy the formula to other cells, these cells are relative references.

6. absolute reference

7. Windows clipboard

8. Double-click the sheet tab, then type the new name, and then press the Enter key or click any cell in the worksheet to accept the entry.

9. Order of precedence is a set of predefined rules that Excel uses to unambiguously calculate a formula by determining which part of the formula to calculate first, which part second, and so on.

Session 2.2

1. Syntax specifies the set of rules that determine the order and punctuation of formulas and functions in Excel.

2. MAX is the function name; A1:A8 is the argument.

3. Assuming you are entering a formula with a function, first select the cell where you want to place a formula, type =, the function name and a left parenthesis, and then click and drag over the range of cells to be used in the formula. Press the Enter key.

4. Click any cell in the row above which you want to insert a row. Click Insert, then click Rows.

5. c

6. select

7. AutoFormat

8. header

9. comment indicator, comment

10. Click Tools, click Options, and then in the View tab, click the Formula check box.

11. landscape

OBJECTIVES

In this tutorial you will:

- Format data using the Number, Currency, Accounting, and Percentage formats

- Align cell contents

- Center text across columns

- Change fonts, font style, and font size

- Clear formatting from cells

- Delete cells from a worksheet

- Use borders and color for emphasis

- Add text box and graphics to a worksheet using the Drawing toolbar

- Remove gridlines from the worksheet

- Print in landscape orientation

- Hide and unhide rows and columns

DEVELOPING A PROFESSIONAL-LOOKING WORKSHEET

Producing a Projected Sales Report for the Pronto Salsa Company

CASE

Pronto Salsa Company

Anne Castelar owns the Pronto Salsa Company, a successful business located in the heart of Tex-Mex country. She is working on a plan to add a new product, de Chili Guero Four-Alarm Red Hot, to Pronto's gourmet salsa line.

Anne wants to take out a bank loan to purchase additional food-processing equipment to handle the requirements of the increased salsa production. She has an appointment with her loan officer at 2:00 p.m. today. To prepare for the meeting, Anne creates a worksheet to show the projected sales of the new salsa and the expected effect on profits. Although the numbers and formulas are in place on the worksheet, Anne has no time to format the worksheet to create the greatest impact. She planned to do that now, but an unexpected problem with today's produce shipment requires her to leave the office for a few hours. Anne asks you to complete the worksheet. She shows you a printout of the unformatted worksheet and explains that she wants the finished worksheet to look very professional—like those you see in business magazines. She also asks you to make sure that the worksheet emphasizes the profits expected from sales of the new salsa.

SESSION 3.1

In this session you will learn how to make your worksheets easier to understand through various formatting techniques. You will format values using Currency, Number, and Percentage formats. You will also change font styles and font sizes, and change the alignment of data within cells and across columns. As you perform all these tasks, you'll find the Format Painter button an extremely useful tool.

Opening the Workbook

After Anne leaves, you develop the worksheet plan in Figure 3-1 and the worksheet format plan in Figure 3-2.

| Figure 3-1 | PLANNING ANALYSIS WORKSHEET |

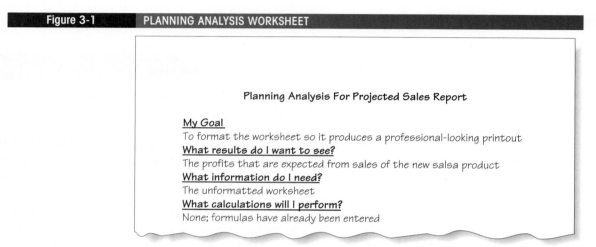

Planning Analysis For Projected Sales Report

My Goal
To format the worksheet so it produces a professional-looking printout
What results do I want to see?
The profits that are expected from sales of the new salsa product
What information do I need?
The unformatted worksheet
What calculations will I perform?
None; formulas have already been entered

| Figure 3-2 | FORMAT PLAN |

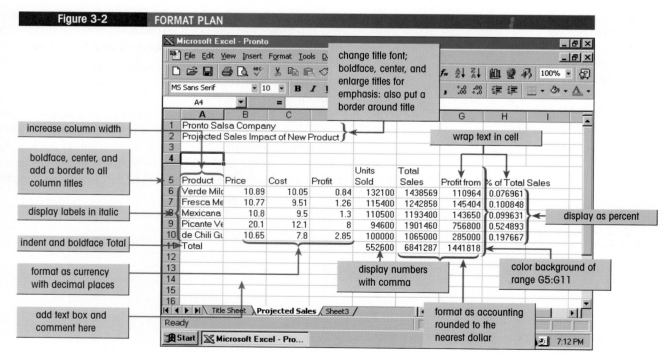

Anne has already entered all the formulas, numbers, and labels. Your main task is to format this information so it is easy to read and understand, and appears professional. This can be accomplished on two levels—by formatting the detailed data in the worksheet and by enhancing the appearance of the worksheet as a whole.

On the data level, you decide that the numbers should be formatted according to their use. For example, the product prices need to appear as dollar values, the column and row labels need to fit within their cells, and the labels need to stand out more. To enhance the worksheet as a whole, you need to structure it so that related information is visually grouped together using lines and borders. Anne also wants certain areas of the worksheet containing key information to stand out, color may be a useful tool for this.

With all that needs to be done before Anne's 2:00 p.m. meeting, you decide that the best place to begin is with formatting the data within the worksheet. Once that is done, you will work to improve the worksheet's overall organization and appearance.

Now that the planning is done, you are ready to start Excel and open the workbook of unformatted data that Anne created.

To start Excel and organize your desktop:

1. Start Excel as usual.

2. Make sure your Data Disk is in the appropriate disk drive.

3. Make sure the Microsoft Excel and Book1 windows are maximized.

Now you need to open Anne's file and begin formatting the worksheet. Anne stored the workbook as Pronto, but before you begin to change the workbook, save it using the filename Pronto Salsa Company. This way, the original workbook, Pronto, remains unchanged in case you want to work through this tutorial again.

To open the Pronto workbook and save the workbook as Pronto Salsa Company:

1. Click the **Open** button 📂 on the Standard toolbar to open the Open dialog box.

2. Open the Pronto workbook in the Tutorial folder for Tutorial 3 on your Data Disk.

3. Click **File** on the menu bar, and then click **Save As** to open the Save As dialog box.

4. In the File name text box, change the filename to **Pronto Salsa Company**.

5. Click the **Save** button 💾 to save the workbook under the new filename. The new filename, Pronto Salsa Company, appears in the title bar.

   TROUBLE? If you see the message "Replace existing file?", click the Yes button to replace the old version of Pronto Salsa Company with your new version.

6. Click the **Projected Sales** sheet tab. See Figure 3-3.

Figure 3-3	PRONTO SALSA COMPANY WORKSHEET

	A	B	C	D	E	F	G	H	I	J	K	L
1	Pronto Salsa Company											
2	Projected Sales Impact of New Product											
3												
4												
5	Product	Price	Cost	Profit	Units Sold	Total Sales	Profit from	% of Total Sales				
6	Verde Mild	10.89	10.05	0.84	132100	1438569	110964	0.076961				
7	Fresca Me	10.77	9.51	1.26	115400	1242858	145404	0.100848				
8	Mexicana	10.8	9.5	1.3	110500	1193400	143650	0.099631				
9	Picante Ve	20.1	12.1	8	94600	1901460	756800	0.524893				
10	de Chili Gu	10.65	7.8	2.85	100000	1065000	285000	0.197667				
11	Total				552600	6841287	1441818					
12												
13												

Studying the worksheet, you notice that the numbers are difficult to read. You decide to improve the appearance of the numbers in worksheet cells first.

Formatting **Worksheet Data**

Formatting is the process of changing the appearance of the data in worksheet cells. Formatting can make your worksheets easier to understand, and draw attention to important points.

In the previous tutorial you used AutoFormat to improve the appearance of your worksheet. AutoFormat applies a predefined format to a selected range in a worksheet. AutoFormat is easy to use, but its predefined format might not suit every application. If you decide to customize a worksheet's format, you can use the extensive Excel formatting options. When you select your own formats, you can format an individual cell or a range of cells.

Formatting changes only the appearance of the worksheet; it does not change the text or numbers stored in the cells. For example, if you format the number .123653 using a Percentage format that displays only one decimal place, the number appears in the worksheet as 12.4%; however, the original number, .123653, remains stored in the cell. When you enter data into cells, Excel applies an automatic format, referred to as the General format. The **General format** aligns numbers at the right side of the cell, uses a minus sign for negative values, and displays numbers without trailing zeros to the right of the decimal point. You can change the General format by using AutoFormat, the Format menu, the Shortcut menu, or toolbar buttons.

There are many ways to access the Excel formatting options. The Format menu provides access to all formatting commands.

The Shortcut menu provides quick access to the Format dialog box. To display the Shortcut menu, make sure the pointer is positioned within the range you have selected to format, and then click the right mouse button.

The Formatting toolbar contains formatting buttons, including the style and alignment buttons, and the Font Style and Font Size boxes, as shown in Figure 3-4.

Figure 3-4	FORMATTING TOOLBAR

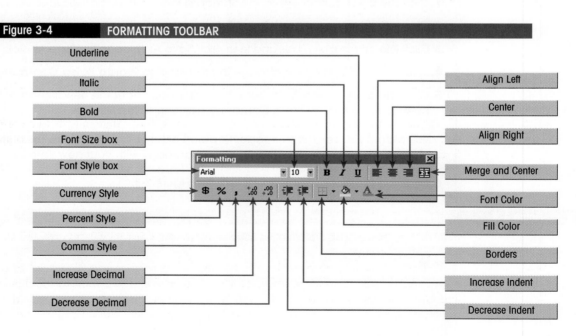

Most experienced Excel users develop a preference for which menu or buttons they use to access the Excel formatting options; however, most beginners find it easy to remember that all formatting options are available from the Format menu.

Looking at Anne's worksheet, you decide to change the appearance of the numbers first.

To center the worksheet titles across columns A through H:

1. Select the range **A1:H2**.

2. Click **Format**, click **Cells**, and then, if necessary, click the **Alignment** tab in the Format Cells dialog box.

3. Click the arrow next to the **Horizontal** text alignment list box to display the horizontal text alignment options.

4. Click the **Center Across Selection** option to center the title lines across columns A through H.

5. Click the **OK** button.

6. Click any cell to deselect the range. See Figure 3-16.

| Figure 3-16 | WORKSHEET WITH TITLES CENTERED ACROSS SEVERAL COLUMNS |

cell contents centered across columns A through H →

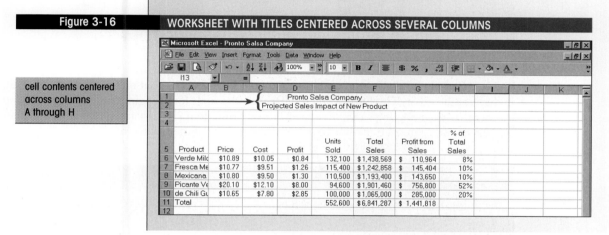

Indenting Text Within a Cell

When you type text in a cell it is left-aligned. You can indent text from the left edge by using the Increase Indent button on the Formatting toolbar or the Index spinner button in the Alignment tab of the Format Cells dialog box. You decide to indent the word "Total" to provide a visual cue of the change from detail to summary information.

To indent text within a cell:

1. Click cell **A11** to make it the active cell.

2. Click the **Increase Indent** button 📇 on the Formatting toolbar to indent the word "Total" within the cell.

3. Click the **Save** button 💾 on the Standard toolbar to save the worksheet.

You check your plan and confirm that you selected formats for all worksheet cells containing data and that the data within the cells is aligned properly. The formatting of the worksheet contents is almost complete. Your next task is to improve the appearance of the labels by changing the font style of the title and the column headings.

You decide to use the Bold button on the Formatting toolbar to change some titles in the worksheet to boldface.

Changing **the Font, Font Style, and Font Size**

A font is a set of letters, numbers, punctuation marks, and symbols with a specific size and design. Figure 3-17 shows some examples. A font can have one or more of the following font styles: regular, italic, bold, and bold italic.

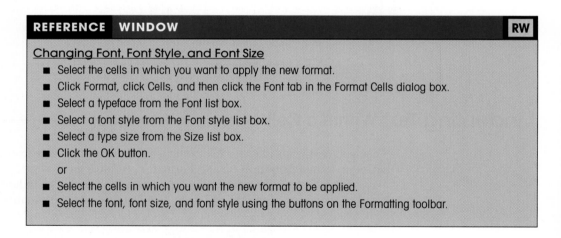

Figure 3-17	SELECTED FONTS			
FONT	**REGULAR STYLE**	**ITALIC STYLE**	**BOLD STYLE**	**BOLD ITALIC STYLE**
Times	AaBbCc	*AaBbCc*	**AaBbCc**	***AaBbCc***
Courier	AaBbCc	*AaBbCc*	**AaBbCc**	***AaBbCc***
Garamond	AaBbCc	*AaBbCc*	**AaBbCc**	***AaBbCc***
Helvetica Condensed	AaBbCc	*AaBbCc*	**AaBbCc**	***AaBbCc***

Most fonts are available in many sizes, and you can also select font effects, such as strikeout, underline, and color. The Formatting toolbar provides tools for changing font style by applying boldface, italics, underline, and increasing or decreasing font size. To access and preview other font effects, you can open the Format Cells dialog box from the Format menu.

REFERENCE WINDOW   **RW**

Changing Font, Font Style, and Font Size
- Select the cells in which you want to apply the new format.
- Click Format, click Cells, and then click the Font tab in the Format Cells dialog box.
- Select a typeface from the Font list box.
- Select a font style from the Font style list box.
- Select a type size from the Size list box.
- Click the OK button.
  or
- Select the cells in which you want the new format to be applied.
- Select the font, font size, and font style using the buttons on the Formatting toolbar.

You begin by formatting the word "Total" in cell A11 in boldface letters.

To apply the boldface font style:

1. If necessary, click cell **A11**.

2. Click the **Bold** button **B** on the Formatting toolbar to set the font style to bold-face. Notice that when a style like bold is applied to a cell's content, the toolbar button appears depressed to indicate that the style is applied to the active cell.

You also want to display the column titles in boldface. To do this, first select the range you want to format, and then click the Bold button to apply the format.

To display the column titles in boldface:

1. Select the range **A5:H5**.

2. Click the **Bold** button **B** on the Formatting toolbar to apply the boldface font style.

3. Click any cell to deselect the range.

Next you want to change the font and size of the worksheet titles for emphasis. You use the Font dialog box (instead of the toolbar) so you can preview your changes. Remember, although the worksheet titles appear to be in columns A through F, they are just spilling over from column A. To format the titles, you need to select only cells A1 and A2—the cells where the titles were originally entered.

To change the font and font size of the worksheet titles:

1. Select the range **A1:A2**. Although the title is centered within the range A1:H2, the values are stored in cells A1 and A2.

2. Click **Format** on the menu bar, and then click **Cells** to open the Format Cells dialog box.

3. Click the **Font** tab. See Figure 3-18.

Figure 3-18   **FONT TAB IN FORMAT CELLS DIALOG BOX**

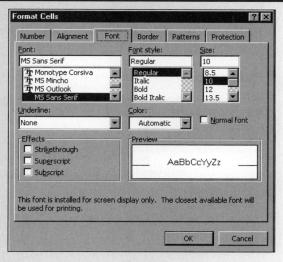

4. Use the Font box scroll bar to find the Times New Roman font. Click the **Times New Roman** font to select it.

5. Click **Bold** in the Font style list box.

6. Click **14** in the Size list box. A sample of the font appears in the Preview box.

7. Click the **OK** button to apply the new font, font style, and font size to the worksheet titles.

8. Click any cell to deselect the titles. See Figure 3-19.

Figure 3-19   **TITLES AFTER NEW FONT, FONT STYLE, AND FONT SIZE APPLIED**

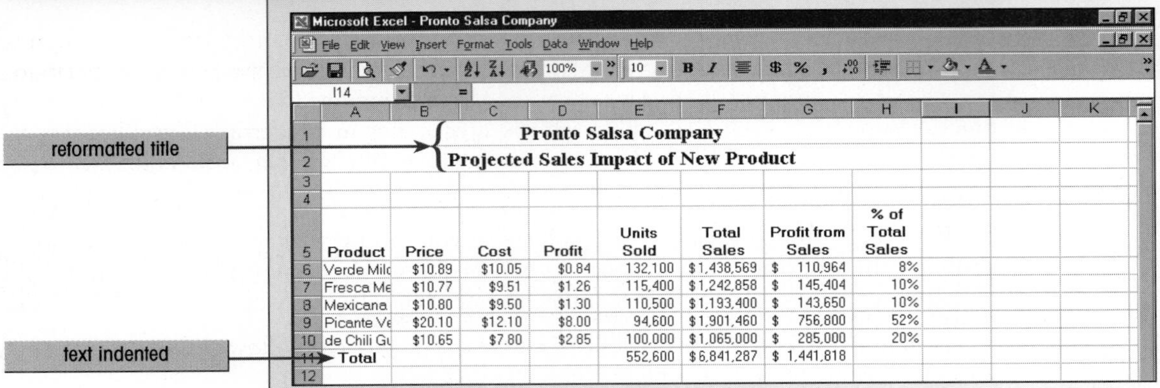

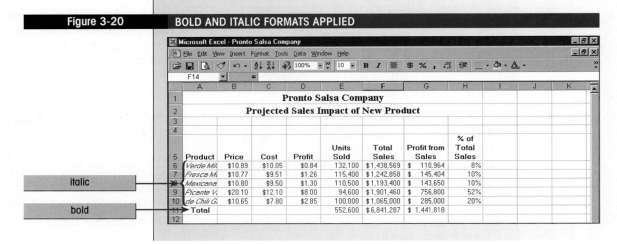

9. Click the **Save** button 🖫 on the Standard toolbar to save the worksheet.

Next you decide to display the products names in italics.

To italicize the row labels:

1. Select the range **A6:A10**.

2. Click the **Italic** button I on the Formatting toolbar to apply the italic font style.

3. Click any cell to deselect the range and view the formatting you have done so far. See Figure 3-20.

Figure 3-20   **BOLD AND ITALIC FORMATS APPLIED**

You hope Anne will approve of the Times New Roman font—it looks like the font on the Pronto salsa jar labels and would like to use it to create a style that can be applied to other worksheets.

Using Styles

A **style** is a saved collection of formatting, such as font, font size, pattern, and alignment that you combine, name and save as a group. A style can include from one to six attributes—Number, font, Alignment, Border, Pattern, and Protection. Once you have saved a style, you can apply it to a cell or range to achieve consistency in formatting. Excel has six predefined styles—Comma, Comma[0], Currency, currency[0], Normal, and Percent. By default, every cell in a worksheet is automatically formatted with the Normal style, which you use whenever you start typing in a new worksheet.

You can create a style in two ways: by using an example of the cell that has the formats you want associated with the style; or manually, by choosing formats from the Style dialog box and selecting the format you want associated with the style.

Although you won't create a style in this tutorial, you can follow the steps in the reference window if you want to create a style.

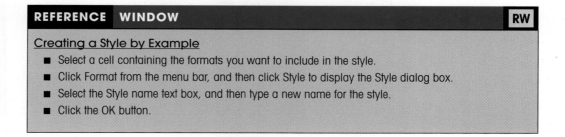

REFERENCE WINDOW   **RW**

Creating a Style by Example
- Select a cell containing the formats you want to include in the style.
- Click Format from the menu bar, and then click Style to display the Style dialog box.
- Select the Style name text box, and then type a new name for the style.
- Click the OK button.

Clearing Formats from Cells

Anne reviews the worksheet and decides the italics format applied to the product names is not necessary. She asks you to remove the formatting from cells A6:A10. Although you could use Undo to remove the last step, you'll use the Edit, Clear command which erases formatting while leaving the cell's content intact. This command can be issued at any time to clear formatting from a cell.

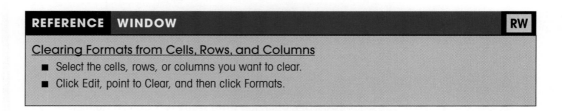

REFERENCE WINDOW   **RW**

Clearing Formats from Cells, Rows, and Columns
- Select the cells, rows, or columns you want to clear.
- Click Edit, point to Clear, and then click Formats.

To clear the formatting of a cell:

1. Select cells A6:A10, the cells whose format you want to clear.

2. Click **Edit**, point to **Clear** and then click **Formats** to return the cell to its default (General) format. Notice the contents of the cells have not been erased.

3. Click any cell to deselect and view the product names in Regular style.

Deleting Cells from a Worksheet

Anne again reviews the worksheet and decides to remove the Cost data, range C5:C11, from the worksheet. You will use the Delete command from the Edit menu to remove these cells from the worksheet. When you delete one or more cells from a worksheet, you remove the space occupied by these cells and must specify if you want the cells beneath the deleted cells to shift up or the cells to the right of the deleted cells to shift to the left.

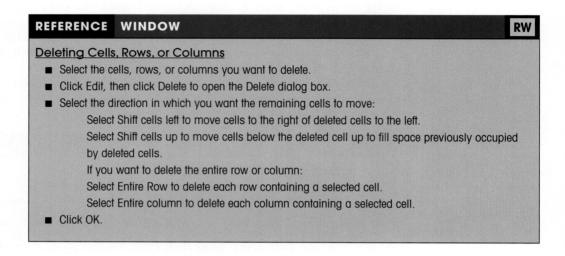

REFERENCE WINDOW   **RW**

Deleting Cells, Rows, or Columns
- Select the cells, rows, or columns you want to delete.
- Click Edit, then click Delete to open the Delete dialog box.
- Select the direction in which you want the remaining cells to move:
      Select Shift cells left to move cells to the right of deleted cells to the left.
      Select Shift cells up to move cells below the deleted cell up to fill space previously occupied by deleted cells.
      If you want to delete the entire row or column:
      Select Entire Row to delete each row containing a selected cell.
      Select Entire column to delete each column containing a selected cell.
- Click OK.

To delete cells from the worksheet

1. Select the range **C5:C11**, the cells to be deleted from the worksheet.

2. Click **Edit**, click **Delete** to open the Delete dialog box .See Figure 3-21.

Figure 3-21   DELETE DIALOG BOX

3. If necessary, click the **Shift cells left** option button.

4. Click OK. Notice all the cells from D5:H6 shift left one column.

5. Click any cell to observe that the Cost data no longer appears in the worksheet. See Figure 3-22. Save the worksheet.

To apply a color to the Profit from Sales column:

1. Select the range **F5:F11**.

2. Click **Format** on the menu bar, click **Cells**, and then click the **Patterns** tab in the Format Cells dialog box. See Figure 3-26. A color palette appears.

Figure 3-26   COLOR PALETTE IN PATTERNS TAB OF FORMAT CELLS DIALOG BOX

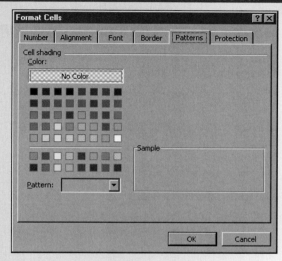

3. Click the **yellow square** in the fourth row (third square from the left) of the Cell shading Color palette.

4. Click the **OK** button to apply the color.

5. Click any cell to deselect the range and view the color in the Profit from Sales column. See Figure 3-27.

Figure 3-27   WORKSHEET AFTER APPLYING COLOR TO A COLUMN

You can also use buttons on the Formatting toolbar to change the color for the cell background (Fill Color button) and text in a cell (Text Color button).

Now that you have finished formatting labels and values, you can change the width of column A to best display the information in that column. To do this, you use Excel's Automatic Adjustment feature to change the width of a column to fit the widest entry in a cell.

To change the column width to fit the contents of a column:

1. Position the pointer over the column boundary between column A and column B. The pointer changes to ↔.

2. Double-click the boundary. The column width automatically adjusts to accommodate the widest entry in column A. See Figure 3-28.

Figure 3-28   **RESULTS OF CHANGING COLUMN WIDTH**

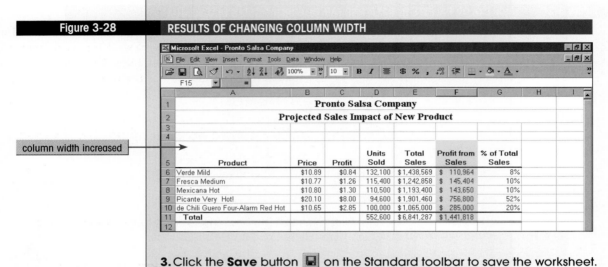

column width increased

3. Click the **Save** button 🖫 on the Standard toolbar to save the worksheet.

Using the Drawing Toolbar for Emphasis

The Excel Text Box feature lets you display notes, comments, and headings in a worksheet. A **text box** is like an electronic Post-it note that appears on top of the worksheet cells.

To add a text box you use the Text Box button, which is located on the Drawing toolbar, and type the note in the text box.

Activating the Drawing Toolbar

Excel provides many toolbars. You have been using two: the Standard toolbar and the Formatting toolbar. Some of the other toolbars include the Chart toolbar, the Drawing toolbar, and the Visual Basic toolbar. To activate a toolbar, it's usually easiest to use the toolbar Shortcut menu, but to activate the Drawing toolbar, you can simply click the Drawing button on the Standard toolbar. When you finish using a toolbar, you can easily remove it from the worksheet.

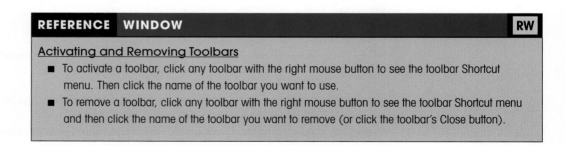

REFERENCE WINDOW   **RW**

Activating and Removing Toolbars
- To activate a toolbar, click any toolbar with the right mouse button to see the toolbar Shortcut menu. Then click the name of the toolbar you want to use.
- To remove a toolbar, click any toolbar with the right mouse button to see the toolbar Shortcut menu and then click the name of the toolbar you want to remove (or click the toolbar's Close button).

You need the Drawing toolbar to accomplish your next formatting task. (If your Drawing toolbar is already active, skip the following step.)

To display the Drawing toolbar:

1. Click the **Drawing** button 📧 on the Standard toolbar.

The toolbar might appear in any location in the worksheet window; this is called a **floating** toolbar. You don't want the toolbar obstructing your view of the worksheet, so drag it to the bottom of the worksheet window to **anchor** it there. (If your toolbar is already anchored at the bottom of the worksheet window, or at the top, skip the next set of steps.)

To anchor the Drawing toolbar to the bottom of the worksheet window:

1. Position the pointer on the title bar of the Drawing toolbar.

2. Click and drag the toolbar to the bottom of the screen.

3. Release the mouse button to attach the Drawing toolbar to the bottom of the worksheet window. See Figure 3-29.

| Figure 3-29 | DRAWING TOOLBAR ATTACHED TO BOTTOM OF WINDOW |

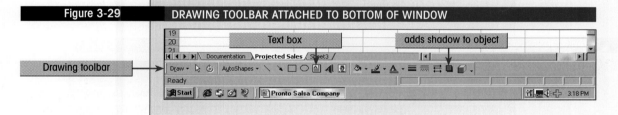

Now that the Drawing toolbar is where you want it, you proceed with your plan to add a comment to the worksheet.

Adding a Text Box

A **text box** is a drawing tool that contains text. It sits on top of the cells in a worksheet and is useful for drawing attention to important points in a worksheet or chart. With Excel you can use a variety of drawing tools, such as boxes, lines, circles, arrows, and text boxes to add graphic objects to your worksheet. To move, modify, or delete a graphic object, you first select it by moving the pointer over the object, then click it. Small square handles indicate that the object is selected. Use these handles to adjust the object's size, change its location, or delete it.

You want to draw attention to the low price and high profit margin of the new salsa product. To do this, you plan to add a text box to the bottom of the worksheet that contains a note about expected profits.

To add a text box:

1. Click the **Text Box** button 📄 on the Drawing toolbar. As you move the pointer inside the worksheet area, the pointer changes to ↓. Position the crosshair of the pointer at the top of cell **A13** to mark the upper-left corner of the text box.

2. Click and drag ╋ to cell **C18**, and then release the mouse button to mark the lower-right corner of the text box. See Figure 3-30.

    You are ready to type the text into the text box.

Figure 3-30   ADDING A TEXT BOX

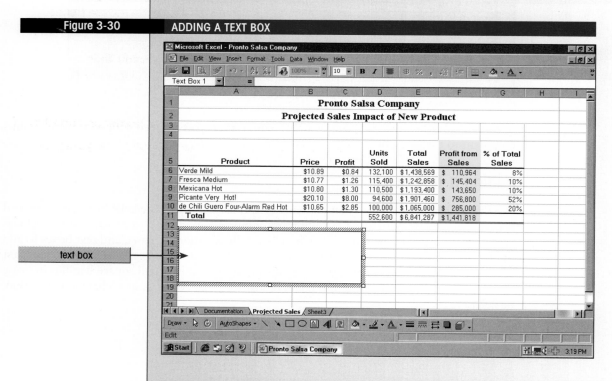

3. Make sure the insertion point is in the text box and then type **Notice the high profit margin of the de Chili Guero Four-Alarm Red Hot. It has the second highest profit per unit.**

You want to use a different font style to emphasize the name of the new salsa product in the text box.

To italicize the name of the new salsa product:

1. Position ⌶ in the text box just before the word "de Chili."

2. Click and drag ⌶ to the end of the word "Hot," and then release the mouse button.

TROUBLE? If the size of your text box differs slightly from the one in the figure, the lines of text might break differently. So don't worry if the text in your text box is not arranged exactly like the text in the figure.

3. Click the **Italic** button ⬚ on the Formatting toolbar.

4. Click any cell to deselect the product name, which now appears italicized.

You decide to change the text box size so that there is no empty space at the bottom.

To change the text box size:

1. Click the **text box** to select it and display the patterned border with handles.

2. Position the pointer on the center handle at the bottom of the text box. The pointer changes to ↕.

3. Click and drag ↕ up to shorten the box, and then release the mouse button.

You want to change the text box a bit more by adding a drop shadow to it.

To add a shadow to the text box:

1. Make sure the text box is still selected. (Look for the patterned border and handles.)

2. Click the **Shadow** button ⬚ on the Drawing toolbar to display the gallery of Shadow options. See Figure 3-31.

Figure 3-31   SHADOW STYLE OPTIONS

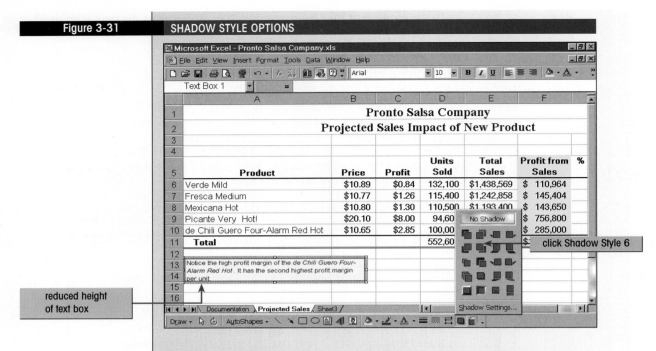

3. Click **Shadow Style 6** (second style from the left in the second row).

4. Click any cell. See Figure 3-32.

Figure 3-32   TEXT BOX WITH SHADOW

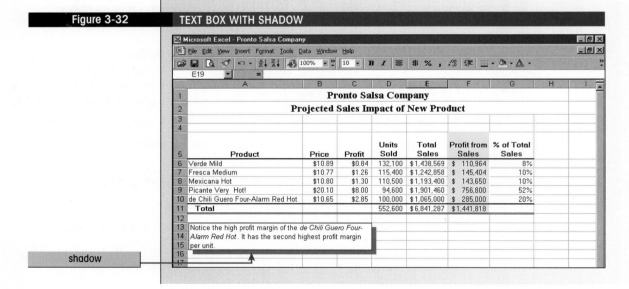

Adding an Arrow

You decide to add an arrow pointing from the text box to the row with information on the new salsa.

To add an arrow:

1. Click the **Arrow** button on the Drawing toolbar. As you move the mouse pointer inside the worksheet, the pointer changes to ╋.

2. Position ╋ on the top edge of the text box in cell **B12**. To ensure a straight line, press and hold the **Shift** key as you drag to cell **B10**, and then release the mouse button.

3. Click any cell to deselect the arrow. See Figure 3-33.

| Figure 3-33 | ADDING AN ARROW |

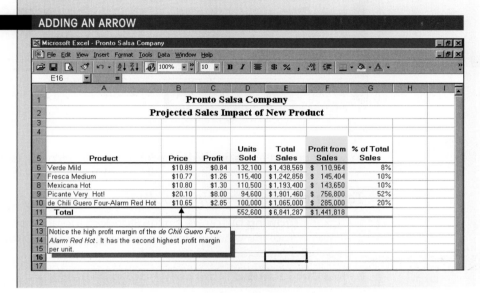

You want the arrow to point to cell C10 instead of B10, so you need to reposition it.

Like a text box, an arrow is an Excel object. To modify the arrow object, you must select it. When you do so, two small square handles appear on it. You can reposition either end of the arrow by dragging one of the handles.

To reposition the arrow:

1. Move the pointer over the arrow object until the pointer changes to ⬉.

2. Click the **arrow**. Handles appear at each end of the arrow.

3. Move the pointer to the top handle on the arrowhead until the pointer changes to ↗.

4. Click and drag ╋ to cell **C10**, and then release the mouse button.

5. Click any cell to deselect the arrow object. See Figure 3-34.

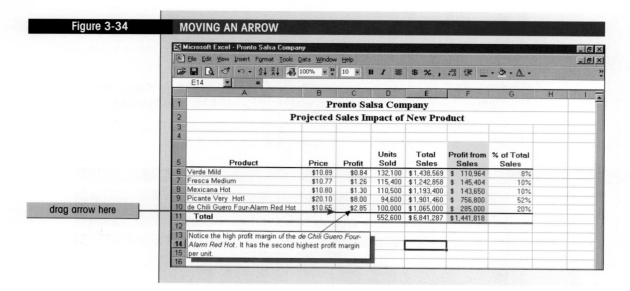

| Figure 3-34 | MOVING AN ARROW |

Now that the text box is finished, you can remove the Drawing toolbar from the worksheet.

To remove the Drawing toolbar:

1. Click the **Drawing** button 🖉 on the Standard toolbar. The Drawing toolbar is removed from the window, and the Drawing button no longer appears depressed (selected).

2. Press **Ctrl + Home** to make cell A1 the active cell.

3. Click the **Save** button 🖫 on the Standard toolbar to save your work.

You have now made all the formatting changes and enhancements to Anne's worksheet. She has just returned to the office, and you show her the completed worksheet. She is very pleased with how professional the worksheet looks, but she thinks of one more way to improve the appearance of the worksheet. She asks you to remove the gridlines from the worksheet display.

Controlling the Display of Gridlines

Although normally the boundaries of each cell are outlined in black, Anne has decided the worksheet will have more of a professional appearance if you remove the gridlines. To remove the gridline display, you deselect the Gridlines option in the View tab of the Options dialog box.

To remove the display of gridlines in the worksheet:

1. Click **Tools** on the menu bar, click **Options**, and if necessary, then click the **View** tab in the Options dialog box.

2. Click the **Gridlines** check box in the Window option to remove the check and deselect the option.

3. Click the **OK** button to display the worksheet without gridlines. See Figure 3-35.

Figure 3-35 **WORKSHEET WITHOUT GRIDLINES**

no gridlines

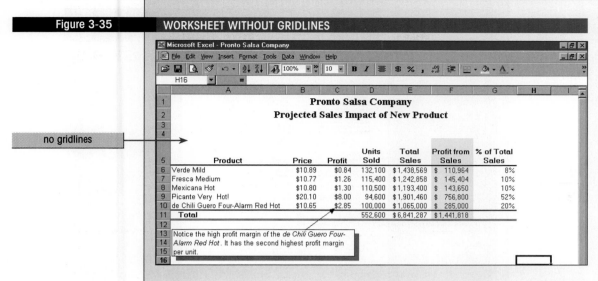

Now you are ready to print the worksheet.

Printing the Worksheet

Before you print a worksheet, you can use the Excel Print Preview window to see how it will look when printed. Recall that the Print Preview window shows you margins, page breaks, headers, and footers that are not always visible on the screen.

To preview the worksheet before you print it:

1. Click the **Print Preview** button on the Standard toolbar to display the first worksheet page in the Print Preview window. See Figure 3-36.

Figure 3-36   PRINT PREVIEW

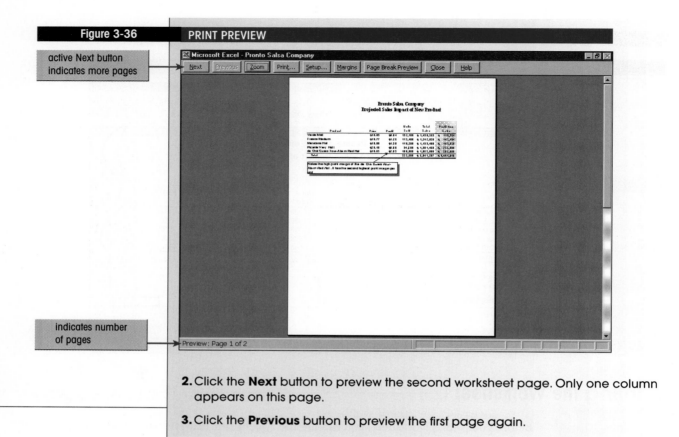

active Next button indicates more pages

indicates number of pages

2. Click the **Next** button to preview the second worksheet page. Only one column appears on this page.

3. Click the **Previous** button to preview the first page again.

Looking at the Print Preview, you see that the worksheet is too wide to fit on a single page. You realize that if you print the worksheet horizontally (lengthwise), it will fit on a single sheet of paper.

Portrait and Landscape Orientations

Excel provides two print orientations, **portrait** and **landscape**. Portrait orientation prints the worksheet with the paper positioned so it is taller than it is wide. Landscape orientation prints the worksheet with the paper positioned so it is wider than it is tall. Because some worksheets are wider than they are tall, landscape orientation is very useful.

You can specify print orientation using the Page Setup command on the File menu or using the Setup button in the Print Preview window. Use the landscape orientation for the Projected Sales worksheet.

To change the print orientation to landscape:

1. In the Print Preview window, click the **Setup** button to open the Page Setup dialog box. If necessary, click the **Page** tab.

2. Click the **Landscape** option button in the Orientation section to select this option.

3. Click the **OK** button to return to the Print Preview window. See Figure 3-37. Notice the landscape orientation; that is, the page is wider than it is tall. The worksheet will now print on one page.

Figure 3-43

Ortiz Marine Service Payroll
Week Ending

Employee	Hours	Pay Rate	Gross Pay	Federal Withholding	State Withholding	Total Deductions	Net Pay
Bramble	16	6					
Juarez	25	6.25					
Smith	30	8					
DiOrio	25	7.75					
Smiken	10	5.90					
Cortez	30	7					
Fulton	20	6					
Total							

Do the following:

1. Create the worksheet sketched in Figure 3-43.

2. Use the following formulas in your workbook to calculate total hours, gross pay, federal withholding, state withholding, total deductions and net pay for the company:
   a. Gross pay is hours times pay rate.
   b. Federal withholding is 15% of gross pay.
   c. State withholding is 4% of gross pay.
   d. Total deductions is the sum of federal and state withholding.
   e. Net pay is the difference between gross pay and total deductions.

3. Apply the formatting techniques learned in this tutorial to create a professional-looking workbook.

4. Assign a descriptive sheet name.

5. Create a Documentation sheet.

6. Save the workbook as **Payroll** in the Cases folder for Tutorial 3.

7. Print the worksheet, including appropriate headers and footers.

8. Remove the hours for the seven employees.

9. Enter the following hours: 18 for Bramble, 25 for Juarez, 35 for Smith, and 20 for DiOrio, 15 for Smiken, 35 for Cortez, and 22 for Fulton.

10. Print the new worksheet.

11. Print the formulas on one page. Include row and column headers in the printed output.

INTERNET ASSIGNMENTS

The purpose of the Internet Assignments is to challenge you to find information on the Internet that you can use to create effective spreadsheets. The actual assignments are updated and maintained on the Course Technology Web site. Log on to the Internet and use your Web browser to go to the Student Online Companion to accompany this text at **www.course.com/NewPerspectives/Office2000**. Click the Excel link, and then click the link for Tutorial 3.

QUICK | CHECK ANSWERS

Session 3.1

1. click Format, click Cells; right-click mouse in cell you want to format; use buttons on the Formatting toolbar

2. **a.** 5.8%   **b.** $0.06

3. Format Painter button

4. The column width of a cell is not wide enough to display the numbers, and you need to increase the column width.

5. Position the mouse pointer over the column header, right-click the mouse and click Column Width. Enter the new column width in the Column Width dialog box. Position the mouse pointer over the right edge of the column you want to modify, and then click and drag to increase the column width.

6. The data in the cell is formatted with the Comma style using two decimal places.

7. center column headings, right-align numbers, and left-align text

8. Left align button, Center button, Right align button, and Merge and Center button

Session 3.2

1. use the Borders tab on the Format Cells dialog box, or the Borders button on the Formatting toolbar

2. click the Drawing button on the Standard toolbar

3. select

4. text box

5. Portrait; landscape

6. drawing object

7. click Tools, click Options, click View tab, and then remove the check from the Gridlines check box

In this tutorial you will:

- Identify the elements of an Excel chart

- Learn which type of chart will represent your data most effectively

- Create an embedded chart

- Move and resize a chart

- Edit a chart

- Change the appearance of a chart

- Place a chart in a chart sheet

- Select nonadjacent ranges

- Work with three-dimensional chart types

- Add a picture to a chart

CREATING CHARTS

Charting Sales Information for Cast Iron Concepts

CASE

Cast Iron Concepts

Andrea Puest, the regional sales manager of Cast Iron Concepts (CIC), a distributor of cast iron stoves, is required to present information concerning sales of the company's products within her territory. Andrea sells in the New England region, which currently includes Massachusetts, Maine, and Vermont. She sells four major models—Star Windsor, Box Windsor, West Windsor, and Circle Windsor. The Circle Windsor is CIC's latest entry in the cast iron stove market. Due to production problems, it was only available for sale the last four months of the year.

Andrea will make a presentation before the director of sales for CIC and the other regional managers next week when the entire group meets at corporate headquarters. Andrea gives you the basic data on sales in her territory for the past year. She must report on both total regional sales and total state sales for each model in her territory. She knows that this kind of information is often understood best when it is presented in graphical form. So she thinks she would like to show this information in a column chart as well as in a pie chart. You help her prepare for her presentation by creating the charts she needs.

SESSION 4.1

In this session you will learn about the variety of Excel chart types and how to identify the elements of a chart. You will learn how to create a column chart and a number of techniques for improving your chart, including moving and resizing it, adding and editing chart text, enhancing a chart title by adding a border, and using color for emphasis.

Excel Charts

Andrea's sales data is saved in a workbook named Concepts. You generate the charts from the data in this workbook.

To start Excel, open the Concepts workbook, and rename it:

1. Start Excel as usual.

2. Open the Concepts workbook in the Tutorial folder for Tutorial 4 on your Data Disk.

   The Documentation sheet appears as the first sheet in the workbook.

3. Type your name and the current date in the appropriate cells in the Documentation sheet.

4. Save the workbook as **Cast Iron Concepts**. After you do so, the new filename appears in the title bar.

5. Click the **Sales Data** tab to move to that sheet. See Figure 4-1.

| Figure 4-1 | SALES DATA WORKSHEET IN CAST IRON CONCEPTS WORKBOOK |

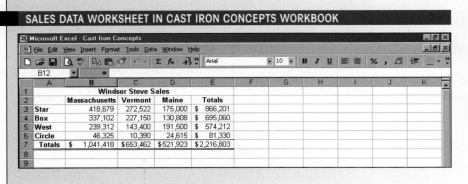

The worksheet shows the annual sales in dollars for each Windsor stove model by state. The total sales during the year for each model are in column E, and the total sales for each state appear in row 7.

It is easy to visually represent this kind of worksheet data. You might think of these graphical representations as "graphs;" however, in Excel they are referred to as **charts**. Figure 4-2 shows the 14 chart types that you can use to represent worksheet data in Excel.

Each chart type has two or more subtypes that provide various alternative chart formats for the selected chart type. For example, the column chart type has seven subtypes, as shown in Figure 4-3.

Figure 4-2   **EXCEL CHART TYPES**

ICON	CHART TYPE	PURPOSE
	Area	Shows magnitude of change over a period of time
	Column	Shows comparisons between the data represented by each column
	Bar	Shows comparisons between the data represented by each bar
	Line	Shows trends or changes over time
	Pie	Shows the proportion of parts to a whole
	XY (Scatter)	Shows the pattern or relationship between sets of (x,y) data points
	Radar	Shows change in data relative to a center point
	Surface	Shows the interrelationships between large amounts of data
	Bubble	A special type of XY (Scatter) that shows the pattern or relationship between sets of data points; compares three sets of data
	Stock	Compares high, low, open, and close prices of a stock
	Cylinder	Shows comparisons between the data represented by each cylinder
	Cone	Shows comparisons between the data represented by each cone
	Pyramid	Shows comparisons between the data represented by each pyramid
	Doughnut	Shows the proportion of parts to a whole

Figure 4-3   **CHART SUBTYPES FOR COLUMN CHART TYPE**

CHART SUBTYPE ICON	DESCRIPTION
	Clustered column
	Stacked column
	100% stacked column
	Clustered column with 3-D visual effect
	Stacked column with 3-D visual effect
	100% stacked column with 3-D visual effect
	3-D column

Figure 4-4 shows the elements of a typical Excel chart. Understanding the Excel chart terminology is particularly important so you can successfully construct and edit charts.

Figure 4-4   **EXCEL CHART ELEMENTS**

The entire chart and all its elements are contained in the **chart area**. The **plot area** is the rectangular area defined by the axes, with the Y-axis forming the left side and the X-axis forming the base; in Figure 4-4 the plot area is in gray. The **axis** is a line that borders one side of the plot area, providing a frame for measurement or comparison in a chart. Data values are plotted along the **value** or **Y-axis**, which is typically vertical. Categories are plotted along the **category** or **X-axis**, which is usually horizontal. Each axis in a chart can have a title that identifies the scale or categories of the chart data; in Figure 4-4 the **X-axis title** is "Territories" and the **Y-axis** title is "Sales ($U.S.)." The chart title identifies the chart.

A **tick mark label** identifies the categories, values, or series in the chart. **Tick marks** are small lines that intersect an axis, like divisions on a ruler, and represent the scale used for measuring values in the chart. Excel automatically generates this scale based on the values selected for the chart. **Gridlines** extend the tick marks on a chart axis to make it easier to see the values associated with the data markers. The **category names** or **category labels**, usually appearing on the X-axis, correspond to the labels you use for the worksheet data.

A **data point** is a single value originating from a worksheet cell. A **data marker** is a graphic representing a data point in a chart; depending on the type of chart, a data marker can be a bar, column, area, slice, or other symbol. For example, sales of the Star Windsor stove in Massachusetts (value 418,679 in cell B3 of the worksheet on your screen) is a data point. Each column in the chart in Figure 4-4 that shows the sales of Windsor stoves is a data marker. A **data series** is a group of related data points, such as the Star Windsor sales shown as red column markers in the chart.

When you have more than one data series, your chart will contain more than one set of data markers. For example, Figure 4-4 has three data series, one for each type of Windsor stove. When you show more than one data series in a chart, it is a good idea to use a **legend** to identify which data marker represents each data series.

Placement of Charts

Charts can be placed in the same worksheet as the data; this type of chart is called an **embedded chart** and enables you to place the chart next to the data so it can easily be reviewed and printed on one page. You can also place a chart in a separate sheet, called a **chart sheet**, which contains only one chart and doesn't have rows and columns. In this tutorial you create both an embedded chart and a chart that resides in a separate chart sheet.

Planning a Chart

Before you begin creating a chart you should plan it. Planning a chart includes the following steps:

- identifying the data points to be plotted, as well as the labels representing each data series and categories for the X-axis
- choosing an appropriate chart type
- sketching the chart, including data markers, axes, titles, labels, and legend
- deciding on the location of the chart within the workbook

Remember, Andrea wants to compare sales for each model in each state in which she sells. She thinks that a column chart is the best way to provide her audience with an accurate comparison of sales of Windsor stoves in her New England territory. She also needs to show sales of each stove model as a percentage of total sales. A pie chart is most effective when showing the size of each part as a percentage of a whole, so she will create a pie chart to use in her presentation as well.

Andrea sketched the column chart and pie chart shown in Figure 4-5.

Figure 4-5	SKETCH OF COLUMN AND PIE CHARTS

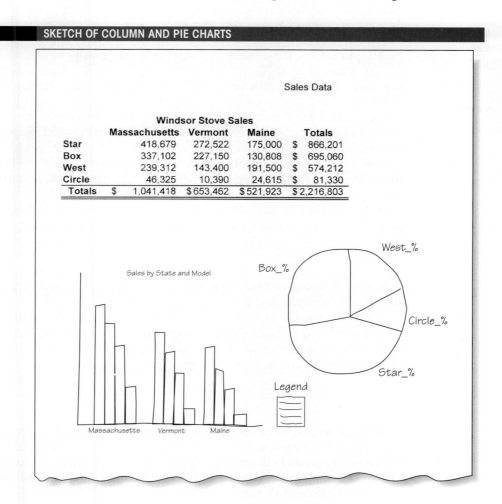

The sketches show roughly how Andrea wants the charts to look. It is difficult to envision exactly how a chart will look until you know how the data series looks when plotted; therefore, you don't need to incorporate every detail in the chart sketch. As you construct the charts, you can take advantage of Excel previewing capabilities to try different formatting options until your charts look just the way you want.

Create the column chart first. In looking at the sketch for this chart, note that Andrea wants to group the data by states; that is, the four models are shown for each of the three states. The names of the states in cells B2:D2 of the worksheet will be used as category labels. The names of each stove model, in cells A3:A6, will represent the legend text. The data series for the chart are in rows B3:D3, B4:D4, B5:D5, and B6:D6.

Creating a Column Chart

After studying Andrea's sketch for the column chart, you are ready to create it using the Sales Data worksheet. When you create a chart, you first select the cells that contain the data you want to appear in the chart and then you click the Chart Wizard button on the Standard toolbar. The Chart Wizard consists of four dialog boxes that guide you through the steps required to create a chart. Figure 4-6 identifies the tasks you perform in each of the Chart Wizard dialog boxes.

Figure 4-6	TASKS PERFORMED IN EACH STEP OF THE CHART WIZARD
DIALOG BOX	**TASKS PERFORMED**
Chart Type	Select the type of chart you want to create—lists the chart types available in Excel; for each chart type, presents you with several chart subtypes from which you can choose
Chart Source Data	Specify the worksheet cells that contain the data and labels that will appear in the chart
Chart Options	Change the look of the chart by changing options that affect the titles, axes, gridlines, legends, data labels, and data tables
Chart Location	Specify where to place the chart: embedded in a worksheet along with the worksheet data, or in a separate sheet called a chart sheet

You know that Andrea intends to create a handout of the worksheet and chart, so you want to embed the column chart in the same worksheet as the sales data, making it easier for her to create a one-page handout.

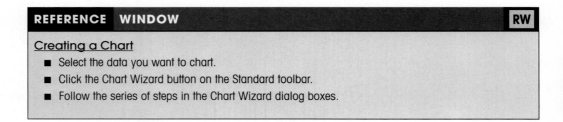

REFERENCE WINDOW   **RW**

Creating a Chart
- Select the data you want to chart.
- Click the Chart Wizard button on the Standard toolbar.
- Follow the series of steps in the Chart Wizard dialog boxes.

Before activating the Chart Wizard, you need to select the cells containing the data the chart will depict. If you want the column and row labels to appear in the chart, include the cells that contain them in your selection as well. For this chart, select the range A2 through D6, which includes the sales of each Windsor stove model in the three states as well as names of the stove models and states.

To create the column chart using the Chart Wizard:

1. Select cells **A2:D6**, making sure no cells are highlighted in column E or row 7. Notice the totals are not included in the range. To include the totals along with the data points that make up totals in the same chart would make the comparison more difficult and might result in a misinterpretation of the data.

   Now that you have selected the chart range, you use the Chart Wizard to create the column chart.

2. Click the **Chart Wizard** button 📊 on the Standard toolbar to open the Chart Wizard - Step 1 of 4 - Chart Type dialog box. See Figure 4-7.

   TROUBLE? If the Office Assistant appears on your screen, click the button next to the message "No, don't provide help now" to close the Office Assistant.

   This first dialog box asks you to select the type of chart you want to create. The Chart type list box lists each of the 14 chart types available in Excel. The default chart type is the Column chart type. To the right of the Chart type list box is a gallery of chart subtypes for the selected chart. Select the chart type you want to create.

| Figure 4-7 | CHART WIZARD STEP 1 OF 4 - CHART TYPE DIALOG BOX |

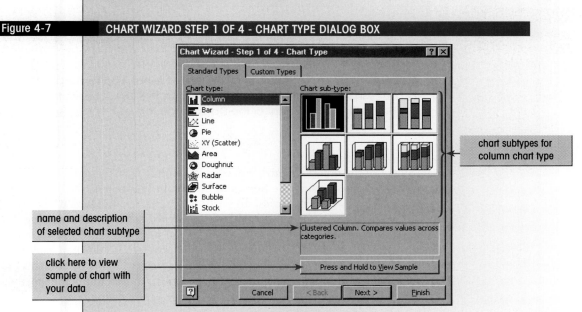

You want to create a column chart.

3. If necessary, click the **Column** chart type (the default) to select it. Seven Column chart subtypes, preformatted chart designs for the column chart, appear. The Clustered Column chart subtype is the default subtype for the Column chart type. Click and hold the **Press and Hold to View Sample** button to see a preview of the Clustered Column chart subtype.

   To view any other Column chart subtype, select another subtype option and click the **Press and Hold to View Sample** button. If you select a different chart type, you will see a different set of subcharts.

   You decide to use the Clustered Column chart type, the default selection.

4. Click the **Next** button to open the Chart Wizard - Step 2 of 4 - Chart Source Data dialog box. See Figure 4-8. In this step you confirm or specify the worksheet cells that contain the data and labels to appear in the chart.

| Figure 4-8 | CHART WIZARD - STEP 2 OF 4 - CHART SOURCE DATA DIALOG BOX |

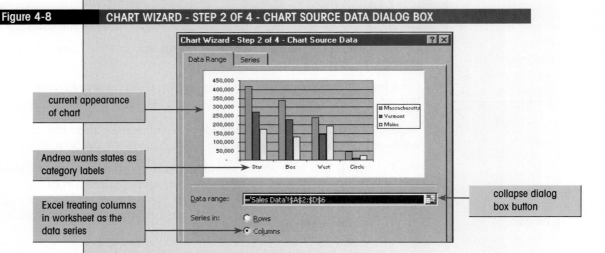

5. Make sure the Data range text box shows "='Sales Data'!$A$2:$D$6." This dialog box provides a preview of your chart.

TROUBLE? If the range shown on your screen is not ='Sales Data'!$A$2:$D$6, type the necessary corrections in the Data range text box, or click the Collapse dialog box button to the right of the Data range text box and select the correct range in the worksheet.

In Step 2 of the Chart Wizard, you can also modify how the data series is organized—by rows or by columns—using the **Series in** option. In Figure 4-8, the chart uses the columns in the worksheet as the data series. To see how the chart would look if the rows in the worksheet were used as the data series, you can modify the settings in this dialog box.

Does the sample chart shown on your screen and in Figure 4-8 look like the sketch Andrea prepared (Figure 4-5)? Not exactly. The problem is that the Chart Wizard assumes that if the range to plot has more rows than columns (which is true in this case), then the data in the columns (states) becomes the data series. Andrea wants the stove models (rows) as the data series, so you need to make this change in the dialog box.

To change the data series and continue the steps in the Chart Wizard:

1. Click the **Rows** option button in the Series in area of the dialog box. The sample chart now shows the stove models as the data series and the states as category labels. See Figure 4-9.

Figure 4-9 **ROWS AS DATA SERIES**

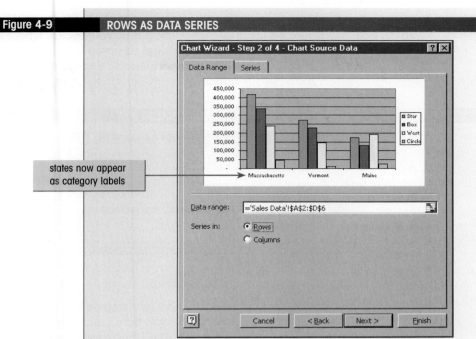

states now appear as category labels

2. Click the **Next** button to open the Chart Wizard - Step 3 of 4 - Chart Options dialog box. See Figure 4-10. A preview area displays the current appearance of the chart. This tabbed dialog box enables you to change various chart options, such as titles, axes, gridlines, legends, data labels, and data tables. As you change these settings, check the preview chart in this dialog box to make sure you get the look you want.

Now add a title for the chart.

Figure 4-10 **CHART WIZARD - STEP 3 OF 4 - CHART OPTIONS DIALOG BOX**

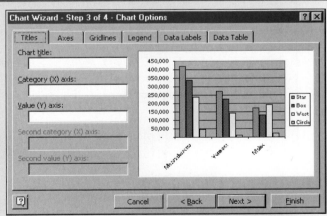

3. If necessary click the **Titles** tab, click the **Chart title** text box, and then type **Sales by State** for the chart title. Notice that the title appears in the preview area.

4. Click the **Next** button to display the Chart Wizard - Step 4 of 4 - Chart Location dialog box. See Figure 4-11. In this fourth dialog box, you decide where to place the chart. You can place a chart in a worksheet as an embedded chart, or place it in its own chart sheet. You want to embed this chart in the Sales Data worksheet, which is the default option.

| Figure 4-11 | CHART WIZARD - STEP 4 OF 4 - CHART LOCATION DIALOG BOX |

You have finished the steps in the Chart Wizard.

5. Click the **Finish** button to complete the chart and display it in the Sales Data worksheet. See Figure 4-12. Notice the selection handles around the chart; these handles indicate that the chart is selected. The Chart toolbar automatically appears when the chart is selected. Figure 4-13 describes each button on the chart toolbar. Also, notice that the data and labels for the chart are outlined in blue, green, and purple in the worksheet. This enables you to quickly see which cells make up the chart.

TROUBLE? If you don't see the Chart toolbar, click View on the menu bar, click Toolbars, and then click the Chart check box to select that option.

| Figure 4-12 | COMPLETED COLUMN CHART |

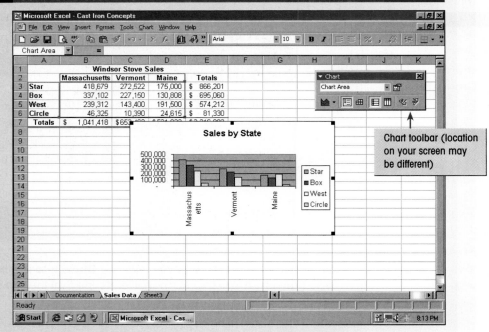

Figure 4-13	DESCRIPTION OF CHART TOOLBAR ELEMENTS	
ICON	**NAME**	**DESCRIPTION**
Chart Area ▾	Chart objects	Drop-down list shows all selectable objects on chart
🖼	Format objects	Displays the Format dialog box for whatever object is selected
📊	Chart type	Drop-down list provides a list of different types of charts
📑	Legend	An on/off toggle to add or remove a legend in a chart
📊	Data Table	An on/off toggle to add or remove a data table in a chart
📊 📊	By Row / By Column	Determines whether the chart's data series is arranged using rows or columns; toggles between the two options.
✎ ✎	Angle Text Downward / Angle Text Upward	45-degree down or 45-degree up angles. Each is a toggle between 45-degree angle and no angle.

6. Click anywhere outside the chart to deselect it. Notice that the selection handles no longer surround the chart, indicating that the chart is no longer selected, and the Chart toolbar is no longer visible. The Chart toolbar only appears when the chart is selected.

After reviewing the column chart, you think that the area outlined for the chart is too small to highlight the comparison between models. You also note that you need to move the chart so that it does not cover the worksheet data.

Moving and Resizing a Chart

When you use the Chart Wizard to create an embedded chart, Excel displays the chart in the worksheet. The size of the chart may not be large enough to accentuate relationships between data points or display the labels correctly. Because a chart is an object, you can move, resize, or copy it like any object in the Windows environment. However, before you can move, resize, or copy a chart, you must select, or **activate** it. You select a chart by clicking anywhere within the chart area. Small black squares, called **selection handles** or **sizing handles**, appear on the boundaries of the chart, indicating that it is selected. You will also notice that some of the items on the menu bar change to enable you to modify the chart instead of the worksheet.

You decide to move and resize the chart before showing it to Andrea.

To change the size and position of the chart:

1. Click anywhere within the white area of the chart border to select the chart. Selection handles appear on the chart border.

TROUBLE? If the Name box does not display the name "Chart Area," click the Chart Objects list box arrow on the Chart toolbar to display the list of chart objects. Select Chart Area.

TROUBLE? If the Chart toolbar is in the way, click and drag it to the bottom of the window to anchor it there.

2. Position the pointer anywhere on the chart border. Click and hold down the mouse button (the pointer changes to ✛) as you drag the chart down and to the left until you see the upper-left corner of the dashed outline in column A of row 8. Release the mouse button to view the chart in its new position.

Now increase the height and width of the chart.

3. Position the pointer on the bottom, right selection handle. When the pointer changes to ↘, hold down the mouse button (note the pointer now changes to +) and drag the selection handle downward to the right until the chart outline reaches the right edge of column H and row 23. Release the mouse button to view the resized chart. See Figure 4-14.

Figure 4-14	CHART AFTER BEING MOVED AND RESIZED

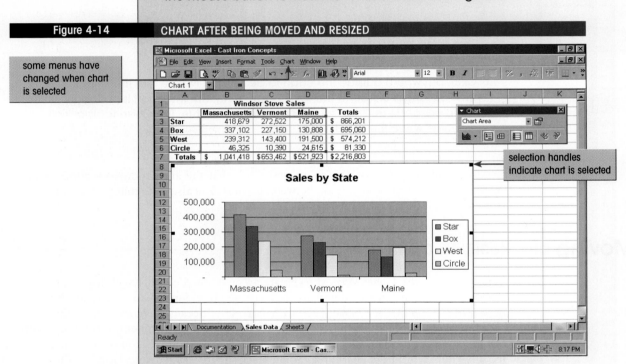

some menus have changed when chart is selected

selection handles indicate chart is selected

4. Click anywhere outside the chart border to deselect the chart. Notice that some of the menus on the menu bar change because the chart is no longer active.

The chart is repositioned and resized. You show Andrea the chart embedded in her Sales Data worksheet. As she reviews the chart, Andrea notices an error in the value entered for West Windsor stoves sold in Maine.

Updating a Chart

Every chart you create is linked to the worksheet data. As a result, if you change the data in a worksheet, Excel automatically updates the chart to reflect the new values. Andrea noticed that sales of West Windsor in Maine were entered incorrectly. She accidentally entered sales as 191,500, when the correct entry should have been 119,500. Correct this data entry error and observe how it changes the column chart.

To change the worksheet data and observe changes to the column chart:

1. Observe the height of the data marker for the West model in Maine (yellow data marker) in the column chart.

2. Click cell **D5**, type **119500**, and then press the **Enter** key. See Figure 4-15. The total West sales (cell E5) and total sales for Maine (cell D7) automatically change. In addition, Excel automatically updates the chart to reflect the new source value. Now the data marker for the West Windsor sales in Maine is shorter.

| Figure 4-15 | MODIFIED COLUMN CHART AFTER CHART'S SOURCE DATA CHANGED |

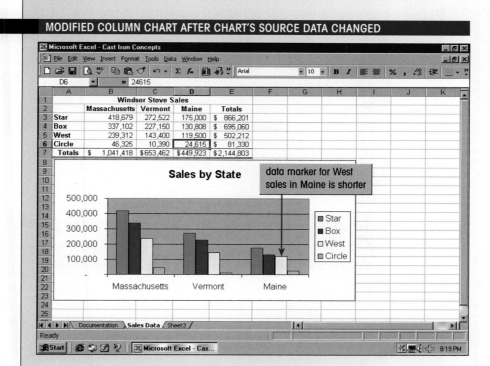

Now that the data for the West stove sales in Maine is corrected, you review the chart with Andrea for ways you can improve the presentation of the chart data.

Modifying an Excel Chart

You can make many modifications to a chart, including changing the type of chart, the text, the labels, the gridlines, and the titles. To make these modifications, you need to activate the chart. Selecting, or activating, a chart, as mentioned earlier, allows you to move and resize it. It also gives you access to the Chart commands on the menu bar and displays the Chart toolbar to use as you alter the chart.

After reviewing the column chart, Andrea believes that the Circle Windsor will distract the audience from the three products that were actually available during the entire period. Recall that the Circle Windsor was only on the market for four months and even then there were production problems. She wants to compare sales only for the three models sold during the entire year.

Revising the Chart Data Series

After you create a chart, you might discover that you specified the wrong data range, or you might decide that your chart should display a different data series. Whatever your reason, you do not need to start over in order to revise the chart's data series.

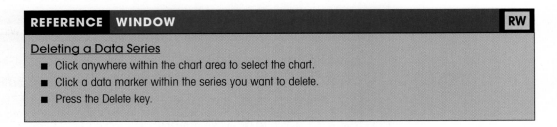

REFERENCE WINDOW   **RW**

Deleting a Data Series
- Click anywhere within the chart area to select the chart.
- Click a data marker within the series you want to delete.
- Press the Delete key.

Andrea asks you to remove the data series representing the Circle Windsor model from the column chart.

To delete the Circle Windsor data series from the column chart:

1. Click anywhere within the chart border to select the chart.

2. Click any data marker representing the Circle data series (any light blue data marker). Selection handles appear on each column of the Circle Windsor data series and a ScreenTip appears identifying the selected chart item. See Figure 4-16.

Figure 4-16   CHART WITH CIRCLE DATA SERIES SELECTED

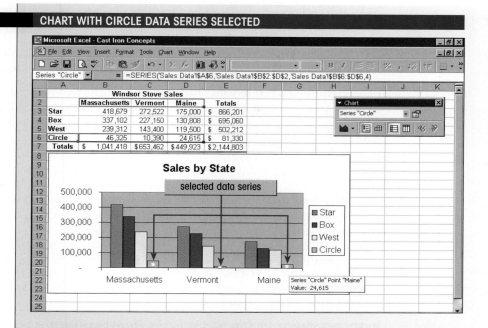

3. Press the **Delete** key. See Figure 4-17. Notice that the Circle Windsor data series disappears from the chart.

Figure 4-17   COLUMN CHART AFTER DATA SERIES REMOVED

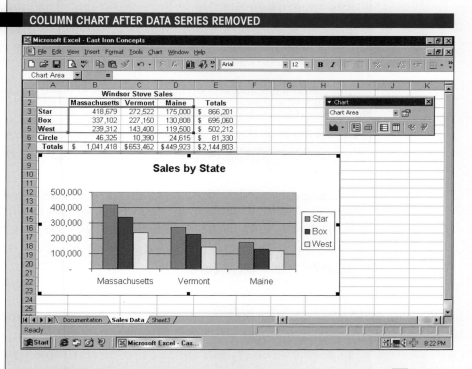

TROUBLE? If you deleted the wrong data series, click the Undo button and then repeat Steps 2 and 3.

Andrea reviews her sketch and notices that the chart title is incomplete; the intended title was "Sales by State and Model." She asks you to make this change to the chart.

Editing Chart Text

Excel classifies the text in your charts in three categories: label text, attached text, and unattached text. **Label text** includes the category names, the tick mark labels, the X-axis labels, and the legend. Label text often derives from the cells in the worksheet; you usually specify it using the Chart Wizard.

Attached text includes the chart title, X-axis title, and Y-axis title. Although attached text appears in a predefined position, you can edit it, and move it using the click-and-drag technique.

Unattached text includes text boxes or comments that you type in the chart after it is created. You can position unattached text anywhere in the chart. To add unattached text to a chart, you use the Text Box tool on the Drawing toolbar.

As noted earlier, you need to change the chart title to "Sales by State and Model." To do this you must select the chart, select the chart title, and then add "and Model" to the title.

To revise the chart title:

1. If the chart is not selected, click the **chart** to select it.

2. Click the **Chart Title** object to select it. Notice that the object name Chart Title appears in the Name box and as a ScreenTip; also, selection handles surround the Chart Title object.

3. Position the pointer in the Chart Title text box at the end of the title, and then click to remove the selection handles from the Chart Title object. The pointer changes to an insertion point I.

   TROUBLE? If the insertion point is not at the end of the title, press the End key to move it to the end.

4. Press the **spacebar**, type **and Model**, and then click anywhere within the chart border to complete the change in the title and deselect it.

Checking Andrea's sketch, you notice that the Y-axis title was not included. To help clarify what the data values in the chart represent, you decide to add "Sales ($U.S.)" as a Y-axis title. You use the Chart Option command on the Chart menu to add this title.

To add the Y-axis title:

1. Make sure that the chart is still selected.

2. Click **Chart** on the menu bar, and then click **Chart Options** to open the Chart Options dialog box. If necessary, click the **Titles** tab.

3. Click the **Value (Y) axis** text box, and then type **Sales ($U.S.)**.

4. Click the **OK** button to close the Chart Options dialog box.

5. Click anywhere within the chart border to deselect the Y-axis title. See Figure 4-18.

4. If necessary, click the **Patterns** tab, click the **Fill Effects** button to open the Fill Effects dialog box, and then click the **Pattern** tab to display the Pattern palette. See Figure 4-21.

Figure 4-21   **PATTERN OPTIONS IN FILL EFFECTS DIALOG BOX**

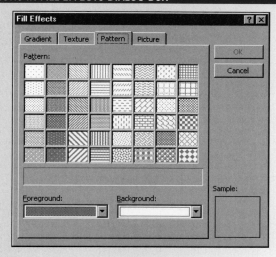

5. Click the **dark downward diagonal** pattern (third row, third column) to select it. Notice that the pattern you selected appears in the Sample box for you to preview.

6. Click the **OK** button to close the Fill Effects dialog box, and then click the **OK** button to close the Format Data Series dialog box and apply the pattern to the Star data series in the chart.

7. Repeat Steps 2 through 6 to select a **narrow horizontal** pattern (fourth row, fourth column) for the Box data series, and again to select a **dark upward diagonal** pattern (fourth row, third column) for the West data series. After you select patterns for the data series, your chart should look like Figure 4-22.

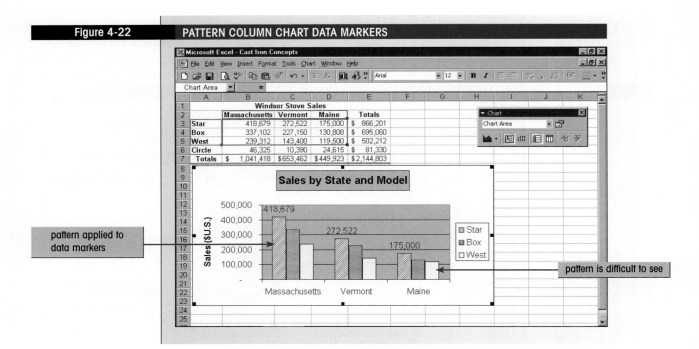

Figure 4-22   **PATTERN COLUMN CHART DATA MARKERS**

pattern applied to data markers

pattern is difficult to see

You notice that the West markers appear to have no pattern applied because the pattern is very difficult to see when applied against the yellow color. You decide to change the color of the West markers to a darker color—green, so the pattern will be more visible.

Instead of changing the color using the Chart toolbar or the Chart menu on the menu bar, you'll use Excel's shortcut menu. Many elements within a chart have a shortcut menu providing context-sensitive commands. To use the shortcut menu, right-click on the chart element and choose a command.

To change the color of data markers:

1. Position the mouse pointer over any West data marker and right-click the mouse button. A shortcut menu appears.

2. Click **Format Data Series** to open the Format Data Series dialog box.

3. If necessary, click the **Patterns** tab, click the **Fill Effects** button, and then click the **Pattern** tab in the Fill Effects dialog box to display the patterns palette.

4. In the Pattern tab, click the **Background** list arrow to display a color palette. Click the **green** square in the third row, third column, and then click the **OK** button to close the Fill Effects dialog box and return to the Format Data Series dialog box.

5. Click the **OK** button to close the Format Data Series dialog box, and then click anywhere outside the chart border to deselect the chart.

You show the chart to Andrea, and she decides that it is ready to be printed and duplicated for distribution at the meeting.

Previewing and Printing the Chart

Before you print you should preview the worksheet to see how it will appear on the printed page. Remember that Andrea wants the embedded chart and the worksheet data to print on one page that she can use as a handout at the meeting.

To save and print an embedded chart:

1. Click the **Save** button on the Standard toolbar to save the workbook.

2. Click the **Print Preview** button on the Standard toolbar to display the Print Preview window.

3. Add your name in the custom footer.

4. Click the **Print** button to open the Print dialog box, and then click the **OK** button. See Figure 4-23.

| Figure 4-23 | PRINTOUT OF WORKSHEET WITH EMBEDDED COLUMN CHART |

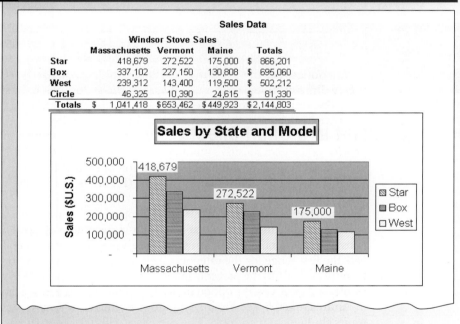

You have finished creating the column chart showing stove sales by state and model for Andrea. Next, you need to create the pie chart showing percentage of total stove sales by model. You will do this in Session 4.2.

Session 4.1 QUICK CHECK

1. A column chart is used to show _____.

2. Explain the difference between a data point and a data marker.

3. What is the purpose of a legend?

4. Describe the action you're likely to take before beginning Step 1 of the Chart Wizard.

5. When you click an embedded chart, it is _____.

6. How do you move an embedded chart to a new location using the mouse?

7. What happens when you change a value in a worksheet that is the source of data for a chart?

8. Explain how to revise a chart's data series.

9. Explain the difference between an embedded chart and a chart.

SESSION 4.2

In this session you will create a pie chart. You will also learn how to select nonadjacent ranges, how to change a two-dimensional pie chart to a three-dimensional pie chart, and how to "explode" a slice from a pie chart. You will also learn how to use chart sheets and how to add a border to a chart.

Creating a Chart in a Chart Sheet

Now Andrea wants to show the contribution of each Windsor model to the total stove sales. Recall from the planning sketch she did (Figure 4-5) that she wants to use a pie chart to show this relationship.

A pie chart shows the relationship, or proportions, of parts to a whole. The size of each slice is determined by the value of that data point in relation to the total of all values. A pie chart contains only one data series. When you create a pie chart, you generally specify two ranges. Excel uses the first range for the category labels and the second range for the data series. Excel automatically calculates the percentage for each slice, draws the slice to reflect the percentage of the whole, and gives you the option of displaying the percentage as a label in the completed chart.

Andrea's sketch (see Figure 4-5) shows estimates of each stove's contribution and how she wants the pie chart to look. The pie chart will have four slices, one for each stove model. She wants each slice labeled with the stove model's name and its percentage of total sales. Because she doesn't know the exact percentages until Excel calculates and displays them in the chart, she put "__%" on her sketch to show where she wants the percentages to appear.

Creating a Pie Chart

You begin creating a pie chart by selecting the data to be represented from the worksheet. You refer to your worksheet and note in the sketch that the data labels for the pie slices are in cells A3 through A6 and the data points representing the pie slices are in cells E3 through E6. You must select these two ranges to tell the Chart Wizard the data that you want to chart, but you realize that these ranges are not located next to each other in the worksheet. You know how to select a series of adjacent cells; now you need to learn how to select two separate ranges at once.

Selecting Nonadjacent Ranges

A nonadjacent range is a group of individual cells or ranges that are not next to each other. Selecting nonadjacent ranges is particularly useful when you construct charts because the cells that contain the data series and those that contain the data labels are often not side by side in the worksheet. When you select nonadjacent ranges, the selected cells in each range are highlighted. You can then format the cells, clear them, or use them to construct a chart.

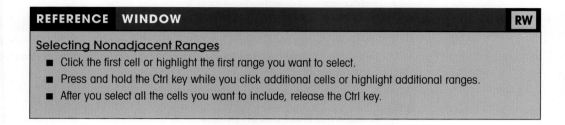

REFERENCE WINDOW   **RW**

Selecting Nonadjacent Ranges
- Click the first cell or highlight the first range you want to select.
- Press and hold the Ctrl key while you click additional cells or highlight additional ranges.
- After you select all the cells you want to include, release the Ctrl key.

Now select the nonadjacent ranges to be used to create the pie chart.

To select range A3:A6 and range E3:E6 in the Sales Data sheet:

1. If you took a break after the last session, make sure that Excel is running, the Cast Iron Concepts workbook is open, and the Sales Data worksheet is open.

2. Click anywhere outside the chart border to make sure the chart is not activated. Press **Ctrl + Home** to make cell A1 the active cell.

3. Select cells **A3** through **A6**, and then release the mouse button.

4. Press and hold the **Ctrl** key while you select cells **E3** through **E6**, and then release the mouse and the Ctrl key. The two nonadjacent ranges are now selected: A3:A6 and E3:E6. See Figure 4-24.

   TROUBLE? If you didn't select the cells you want on your first try, click any cell to remove the highlighting, then go back to Step 2 and try again.

| Figure 4-24 | SELECTING NONADJACENT CELL RANGES |

nonadjacent ranges selected

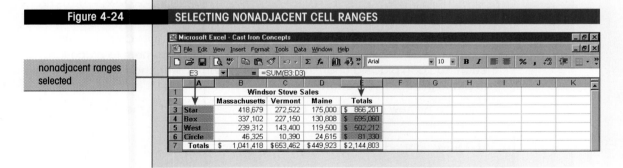

This time you'll place your new chart in a chart sheet, a special sheet that contains only one chart. It does not have the rows and columns of a regular worksheet. If you have many charts to create, you may want to place each chart in a separate chart sheet to avoid cluttering the worksheet. This approach also makes it easier to locate a particular chart because you can change the name on the chart sheet tab.

To create a pie chart in a chart sheet:

1. Click the **Chart Wizard** button [■] on the Standard toolbar to open the Chart Wizard - Step 1 of 4 - Chart Type dialog box.

   TROUBLE? If the Office Assistant appears on your screen, click the button next to the message "No, don't provide help now" to close the Office Assistant.

   You want to create a pie chart.

2. Click the **Pie** chart type to select it. Six Pie chart subtypes appear. The Two-dimensional Pie chart subtype is the default subtype for the Pie chart type. Click the **Press and hold to view sample** button to display a preview of the Pie chart type.

   You decide to use the default chart subtype.

3. Click the **Next** button to open the Chart Wizard - Step 2 of 4 - Chart Source Data dialog box. Make sure the Data range text box displays "='SalesData'!$A$3:$A$6, 'Sales Data'!$E$3:$E$6." This dialog box also displays a preview of your chart.

   TROUBLE? If the range shown on your screen is not "='Sales Data'!$A$3:$A$6, 'Sales Data'!$E$3:$E$6," type the necessary corrections in the Data range text box, or click the Collapse Dialog button located to the right of the Data range text box, and then select the correct range in the worksheet.

4. Click the **Next** button to open the Chart Wizard - Step 3 of 4 - Chart Options dialog box.

   Add a title for the chart.

5. If necessary, click the **Titles** tab, click the **Chart title** text box, and then type **Sales by Model** for the chart title. Notice that the title appears in the preview area.

6. Click the **Data Labels** tab, and then click the **Show label and percent** option button to place the label and percentage next to each slice.

   Now remove the legend because it is no longer needed.

7. Click the **Legend** tab, and then click the **Show legend** check box to remove the check and deselect that option.

8. Click the **Next** button to open the Chart Wizard - Step 4 of 4 - Chart Location dialog box. Recall that in the fourth dialog box you decide where to place the chart. You can place a chart in a worksheet or in its own chart sheet. You want to place this chart in a chart sheet.

9. Click the **As new sheet** option button to place the chart in the Chart1 chart sheet.

   You have finished the steps in the Chart Wizard.

10. Click the **Finish** button to complete the chart. The new chart, along with the Chart toolbar, appears in the chart sheet named Chart1. The chart sheet is inserted into the workbook before the worksheet on which it is based. See Figure 4-25.

Figure 4-25	PIE CHART IN A CHART SHEET

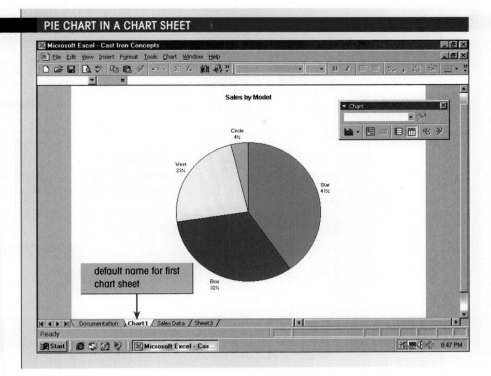

After reviewing the pie chart, Andrea asks you to change the current pie chart to a three-dimensional design to give the chart a more professional look.

Changing the Chart Type from Two-Dimensional to Three-Dimensional

As you recall, Excel provides 14 different chart types that you can choose from as you create a chart. You can also access these chart types after the chart is created and change from one type to another. To change the chart type, you can use the Chart Type command on the Chart menu or the Chart Type button on the Chart toolbar. You use the Chart toolbar to change this two-dimensional pie chart to a three-dimensional pie chart.

> **To change the pie chart to a three-dimensional pie chart:**
>
> 1. Make sure the chart area is selected, and then click the **Chart Type** 📊 ▾ arrow on the Chart toolbar to display a palette of chart types. See Figure 4-26.
>
>   **TROUBLE?** If the Chart toolbar does not appear on the screen, click View on the menu bar, point to Toolbars, and then click the Chart check box to display the Chart toolbar.

Figure 4-26   **PALETTE OF CHART TYPES**

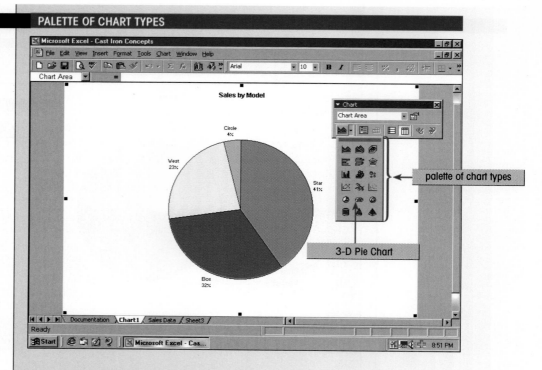

2. Click the **3-D Pie Chart** sample in the fifth row of the second column. The chart reappears as a three-dimensional pie chart. Notice that the Chart Type icon now reflects the new chart type. See Figure 4-27.

Figure 4-27   **THREE-DIMENSIONAL PIE CHART**

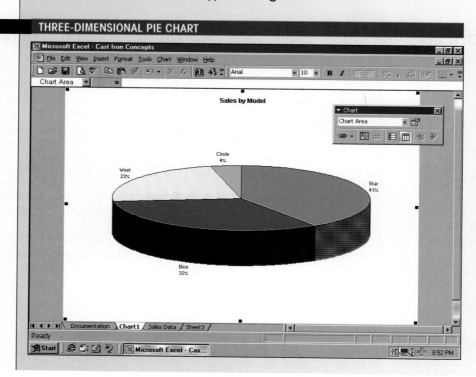

In her presentation, Andrea plans to emphasize the importance of the Star model because it is her best-selling model in the New England territory. She decides to "explode" the Star slice.

Exploding a Slice of a Pie Chart

When you create a pie chart, you may want to focus attention on a particular slice in the chart. You can present the data so a viewer can easily focus attention on one component, for example, which product sold the most. One method of emphasizing a particular slice over others is separating or "exploding" the slice from the rest of the pie. The *cut* slice is more distinct because it is not connected to the other slices. A pie chart with one or more slices separated from the whole is referred to as an exploded pie chart.

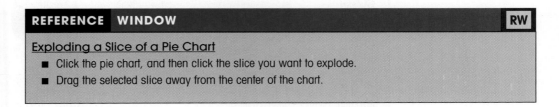

REFERENCE	WINDOW	RW

Exploding a Slice of a Pie Chart
- Click the pie chart, and then click the slice you want to explode.
- Drag the selected slice away from the center of the chart.

Andrea asks you to explode the slice that represents sales for the Star model.

To explode the slice that represents the Star model sales:

1. Click anywhere in the pie chart to select it. One selection handle appears on each pie slice and the Name box indicates that Series 1 is the selected chart object.

2. Now that you have selected the entire pie, you can select one part of it, the Star slice. Position the pointer over the slice that represents Star model sales. As you move the pointer over this slice, the ScreenTip "Series 1 Point: "Star" Value: $866,201 (41%)" appears. Click to select the slice. Selection handles now appear on only this slice.

3. With the pointer on the selected slice, click and hold down the mouse button while dragging the slice to the right, away from the center of the pie chart. As you drag the slice, an outline of the slice marks your progress.

4. Release the mouse button to leave the slice in the new position. See Figure 4-28.

Figure 4-28	PIE CHART WITH EXPLODED SLICE

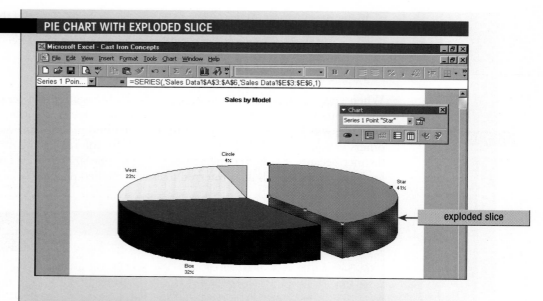

5. Click any white chart area of the pie chart to deselect the exploded slice.

The Star model now is exploded in the pie chart, but Andrea still isn't satisfied. You suggest moving the slice to the front of the pie.

Rotating a Three-Dimensional Chart

When working with a three-dimensional chart, you can modify the view of your chart to change its perspective, elevation, or rotation. You can change the elevation to look down on the chart or up from the bottom. You can also rotate the chart to adjust the placement of objects on the chart. Now rotate the chart so that the Star slice appears at the front of the chart.

> ### To change the three-dimensional view of the chart:
>
> **1.** Click **Chart** on the menu bar, and then click **3-D View** to open the 3-D View dialog box. See Figure 4-29.

Figure 4-29	3-D VIEW DIALOG BOX

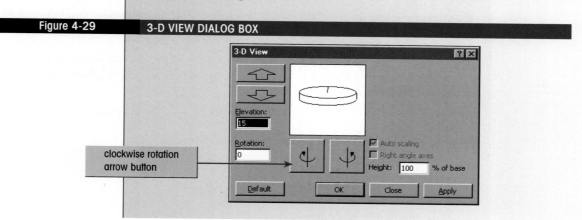

2. Click the **clockwise rotation arrow** button until the Rotation box shows **90**; as you do this, notice that the pie chart sketch in the dialog box rotates to show the new position.

3. Click the **OK** button to apply the changes.

4. Click anywhere in the white area of the chart. See Figure 4-30.

| Figure 4-30 | THREE-DIMENSIONAL PIE CHART AFTER VIEW ROTATED TO DISPLAY CUT SLICE |

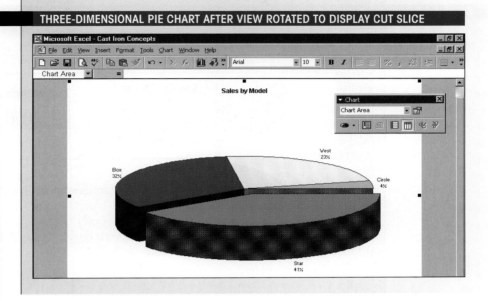

After looking over the chart, you decide to increase the size of the chart labels so that they are easier to read.

Formatting Chart Labels

You can change the font type, size, style, and the color of text in a chart using the Formatting toolbar buttons.

You look at the chart and decide that it will look better if you increase the size of the data labels from 10 to 14 points and apply a bold style to them.

To change the font size and style of the chart labels:

1. Click any one of the four data labels to select all the data labels. Selection handles appear around all four labels, and the Name box displays "Series 1 Data Labels."

2. Click the **Font Size** list arrow on the Formatting toolbar, and then click **14**.

3. Click the **Bold** button on the Formatting toolbar.

Now increase the font size of the title to 20 points.

To change the font size of the chart title:

1. Click the **chart title** to select it. Selection handles appear around the title.

2. Click the **Font Size** list arrow on the Formatting toolbar, and then click **20**.

3. Click any white area of the pie chart to deselect the title. See Figure 4-31.

| Figure 4-31 | THREE-DIMENSIONAL PIE CHART AFTER FONT SIZE OF DATA LABELS AND TITLE INCREASED |

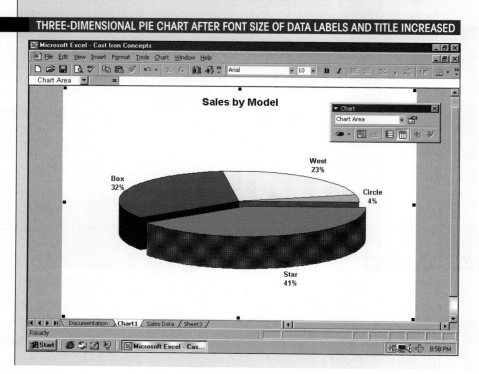

The pie chart looks good but Andrea has one last request. She asks you to apply a blue texture to the chart background.

Applying a Texture Fill Effect to the Chart Background

You can apply texture or gradient fill effects to chart walls, floors, bars, columns, and chart and plot background areas. These fill effects provide a professional look. You want to change the white chart area of the pie chart to a blue texture.

To apply a texture fill effect to the chart background:

1. Make sure the chart area is selected. If it is not, click the white area around the pie chart.

2. Click the **Format Chart Area** button 📑 on the Chart toolbar to open the Format Chart Area dialog box.

3. If necessary, click the **Patterns** tab, click the **Fill Effects** button to open the Fill Effects dialog box, and then click the **Texture** tab. See Figure 4-32.

REVIEW ASSIGNMENTS

Andrea comes to work the next morning and asks you to create one more chart for her presentation. Do the following:

1. Start Windows and Excel, if necessary. Insert your Data Disk into the disk drive. Make sure that the Excel and Book1 windows are maximized. Open the file **Concept2** in the Review folder for Tutorial 4.

2. Save the file under the new name **Cast Iron Concepts 2** in the Review folder.

3. Type your name and the current date in the Documentation sheet.

4. In the Sales Data sheet, select the range that contains the models (A3:D6).

5. Use the Chart Wizard to create a stacked column chart with three-dimensional visual effect.

6. Move the legend to the bottom and add "Total Stove Sales" as the chart title.

7. Place the completed chart in a chart sheet. Rename the chart sheet "Stacked Column".

Explore   8. Put a box around the chart's title, using a thick line for a border. Add a drop shadow.

9. Save the workbook. Print the chart. Include your name, the filename, and the date in the footer.

Explore   10. Select the Walls chart element and apply a one-color gradient fill effect. Select an appropriate color. Also apply a one-color gradient fill effect to the floor chart element. (*Hint:* Move the pointer over the different chart elements to identify the floor and wall elements.)

Explore   11. Select the value axis and change its scale so that the major unit is 150000. (*Hint:* Format the value axis, Scale tab.)

12. Annotate the column chart with the note "Star model our best seller!" by adding a text box and arrow using the tools on the Drawing toolbar.

13. Save the workbook, and then print the stacked bar chart.

14. Open the workbook **ElectronicFilings** and save it as **Filing Solution**.
    a. Prepare an embedded line chart. Add the title "Electronic Filings at the IRS" and the value axis label "Number filed". Remove the legend.
    b. Move and resize the chart until you are satisfied with its appearance.
    c. Change the line weight to the thickest option.
    d. Add a square yellow data marker at each data point.
    e. Save and print the worksheet with the chart.

CASE PROBLEMS

Case 1. Illustrating Production Data at TekStar Electronics   You are an executive assistant at TekStar Electronics, a manufacturer of consumer electronics. You are compiling the yearly manufacturing reports and have collected production totals for each of TekStar's four manufacturing plants. The workbook TekStar contains these totals. You need to create a three-dimensional pie chart showing the relative percentage of CD players each plant produced.

1. Open the workbook **Tekstar** in the Cases folder for Tutorial 4 and add information to the Documentation sheet to create a summary of the workbook. Save the workbook as **TekStar Electronics** in the Cases folder for Tutorial 4.

2. Activate the Units Sold sheet. Use the Chart Wizard to create a three-dimensional pie chart in a chart sheet that shows the percentage of CD players produced at each plant location. Use the Pie with three-dimensional visual effect subtype.

3. Enter "Production of CD Players" as the chart title. Show "Label" and "Percent" as the data labels. Remove the legend.

4. Pull out the slice representing the Chicago plant's CD player production.

5. Increase the font size of the title and data labels so that they are easier to read.

6. Name the chart sheet "3D Pie Chart".

7. Preview and print the chart sheet. Save your work.

8. Create an embedded chart comparing sales of all the products by city. Select the appropriate range and then use the Chart Wizard to create a clustered bar chart. Use the products as the data series and the cities as the X-axis (category) labels. Enter "Production by Product and Plant Location" as the title.

9. Move the bar chart under the table, and then enhance the chart in any way you think appropriate.

10. Preview and print the embedded bar chart, and then save your work.

11. Create a clustered column chart with three-dimensional visual effect comparing the production of VCRs by city. Remove the legend, and then place the chart in a chart sheet named "VCRs".

   a. Add a data table (a grid in a chart that contains the numeric data used to create the chart) to the chart. (*Hint*: Use the Office Assistant to find out how to add a data table to a chart.)

   b. Save the workbook, and then print the chart.

Case 2. Dow Jones Charting   You work for a stock analyst who plans to publish a weekly newsletter. One component of the newsletter will be a 15-week chart tracking the Dow Jones average. Create the chart to be used for the newsletter.

1. Open the workbook **DowJones** in the Cases folder for Tutorial 4. Save the workbook as **Dow Jones Chart** in the Cases folder for Tutorial 4.

2. Use the Chart Wizard to create an embedded line chart (Line subtype) in the Dow Jones worksheet. Specify "Dow Jones Average" as the chart title and "Index" as the title for the Y-axis. Do not add a legend or X-axis title.

3. Place the chart to the right of the present worksheet data and resize it until you are satisfied.

4. Edit the chart as follows:

   a. Change the line marker to a thick line.

   b. Apply a texture fill effect to the chart area. You decide the texture.

   c. Change the color of the plot area. You decide the color.

   Explore   d. Angle the text upward for the dates on the category axis. (*Hint*: Select the category axis and review the buttons on the chart toolbar.)

   e. Change the scale of the Y-axis so the minimum value is 7000.

5. Add your name to a custom footer, and then print the data and the chart.

6. Add the text box with the note "Market roars back to new high" and then insert an arrow pointing from the text box to anywhere between 11/27/98 and 12/11/98.

7. Save your workbook. Print only the chart.

8. The Dow Jones average for the week ending 12/18/98 was 8600.

   a. Insert this data in the row before the 12/11/98 entry.

   Explore   b. Modify the chart by plotting the 15-week period beginning 9/11/98 and ending 12/18/98. (*Hint*: Modify the source data range.)

   Explore   c. Change the location of the chart to a chart sheet. (*Hint*: Check out the Location command on the Chart menu.)

   d. Save the workbook as **Dow Jones 2**, preview your work, and then print the chart.

Case 3. California Chronicle   You work as an intern for Gerry Sindle, business economist, of the *California Chronicle*. The paper plans to publish an economic profile of regions in the state, and you are assisting.

1. Open the workbook **California** in the Cases folder for Tutorial 4. Save the workbook as **California Economic Data**. Create three charts, each in its own chart sheet.

2. Create a pie chart that compares the population of the five geographic areas in the study. Title the chart and enhance it as you think appropriate. Rename the chart sheet to reflect the chart it contains.

3. Create a column chart that compares the number of establishments in retail and services by the five geographic areas. Place the type of establishment on the category axis; each geographic area is a data series. Title the chart and enhance it as you think appropriate. Rename the chart sheet to reflect the chart it contains.

4. Create a bar chart comparing Retail sales and Service receipts by geographic area (categorize by geographic area; the data series is sales and receipts). Title the chart and enhance it as you think appropriate. Rename the chart sheet to reflect the chart it contains.

5. Add a documentation sheet that includes your name, date created, purpose, and a brief description of each sheet in the workbook.

6. Save the workbook.

7. Print the entire workbook (documentation, data worksheet, and the three chart sheets).

Case 4. Association of Realtors   Each year the Association of Realtors collects data on the number of homes sold and the median prices of those sales. Figure 4-37 shows data compiled by the Association since 1987. To better inform the community about occurrences in the home sales market over a ten-year period, the Association wants to release information to the press. Because charts show the data in a more understandable format, the Association has hired you as a part-time analyst to create charts.

Figure 4-37

	Houses Sold	Median Price
1988	4344	$118,500
1989	4294	$127,500
1990	4224	$129,900
1991	3728	$126,000
1992	3477	$123,000
1993	4352	$117,000
1994	4784	$115,300
1995	5081	$115,000
1996	4567	$115,000
1997	5115	$117,000
1998	5199	$117,500

1. Prepare a worksheet using the data from Figure 4-37. (*Hint*: Enter the year as text by typing an apostrophe (') in front of the year.)

2. Create an embedded chart showing the trend in house sales between 1988 and 1998. Title the chart and enhance it as you think appropriate.

3. Create an embedded chart showing the trend in median prices for houses between 1988 and 1998. Title the chart and enhance it as you think appropriate. Print the worksheet including the embedded charts.

Explore

4. Create a chart showing the trend in house sales and median price between 1988 and 1998 (one chart). Place this chart in a chart sheet. Title the chart and enhance it as you think appropriate. (*Hint*: Look up Secondary Value Axis in Help.)

5. The Association of Realtors touted the home sales figures as "shattering all records." Do you agree? Modify the chart in Step 4 by inserting annotated comments supporting or disagreeing with the Association. Print the chart.

6. Save the workbook as **RealtorCharts** in the Cases folder for Tutorial 4.

INTERNET ASSIGNMENTS

The purpose of the Internet Assignments is to challenge you to find information on the Internet that you can use to create effective spreadsheets. The actual assignments are updated and maintained on the Course Technology Web site. Log on to the Internet and use your Web browser to go to the Student Online Companion to accompany this text at **www.course.com/NewPerspectives/office2000**. Click the Excel link, and then click the link for Tutorial 4.

QUICK CHECK ANSWERS

Session 4.1

1. comparison among items or changes in data over a period of time
2. A data point is a value in the worksheet, whereas the data marker is the symbol (pie slice, column, bar, and so on) that represents the data point in a chart.
3. identifies the pattern or colors assigned to the data series in a chart
4. select the range of cells to be used as the source of data for the chart
5. selected; also referred to as activated
6. select the chart, move the pointer over the chart area until the pointer changes to an arrow, and then click and drag to another location on the worksheet
7. The data marker that represents that data point will change to reflect the new value.
8. Select the appropriate chart, click Chart menu, and then Source Data. Click the Collapse dialog box button, select values to be included in the chart, press the Enter key, and then click the OK button.
9. An embedded chart is a chart object placed in a worksheet and saved with the worksheet when the workbook is saved; a chart sheet is a sheet in a workbook that contains only a chart.

Session 4.2

1. pie chart
2. a. a value that originates from a worksheet cell
   b. a slice in a pie chart that represents a single point
   c. a group of related data points plotted in a pie chart that originate from rows or columns in a worksheet
3. often, the data you want to plot is not in adjacent cells
4. select cell A1, press and hold Ctrl key, and then select cells C5 and D10
5. chart type
6. select the slice you want to "explode," and then click and drag the slice away from the center
7. select the pie chart you want to rotate, click Chart on the Menu bar, click 3-D View to open the 3-D View dialog box, and then click one of the rotate buttons to rotate the chart

INDEX

TASK	PAGE #	RECOMMENDED METHOD
AutoComplete, use	EX 1.15	To accept Excel's suggestion, press Enter. Otherwise, continue typing a new label.
AutoFormat, use	EX 2.28	Select the range to format, click Format, then click AutoFormat. Select desired format from Table Format list, then click OK.
AutoSum button, use	EX 2.07	Click the cell where you want sum to appear. Click Σ. Make sure the range address in the formula is the same as the range you want to sum.
Border, apply	EX 3.21	*See* Reference Window: Adding a Border
Cancel action	EX 2.26	Press Esc, or click Undo ↰.
Cell contents, clear	EX 1.29	Select the cells you want to clear, then press Delete.
Cell contents, copy using Copy command	EX 2.10	Select the cell or range you want to copy, then click ▣.
Cell contents, copy using fill handle	EX 2.10	Click cell(s) with data or label to copy, then click and drag the fill handle to outline the cell(s) to which the data is to be copied.
Cell reference types, edit	EX 2.14	Double-click cell containing formula to be edited. Move insertion point to part of cell reference to be changed, then press F4 until reference type is correct, then press Enter.
Chart, activate	EX 4.11	Click anywhere within the chart border. Same as selecting.
Chart, add data labels	EX 4.17	Select the chart, then select a single data marker for the series. Click Chart, click Options, then click Data Labels. Select the type of data labels you want, then click OK.
Chart, adjust size	EX 4.11	Select the chart and drag selection handles.
Chart, apply a pattern to a data marker	EX 4.20	*See* Reference Window: Selecting a Pattern for a Data Marker
Chart, apply a texture	EX 4.32	Click Format Chart Area on Chart toolbar, click Patterns tab, click Fill Effects button, and then click the Texture tab. Select the desired texture.
Chart, create	EX 4.06	Select data to be charted. Click ▦, then complete the steps in the Chart Wizard dialog boxes.
Chart, delete data series	EX 4.14	Select the chart, select the data series, then press Delete.
Chart, explode pie slice	EX 4.29	Select the pie chart, then click the slice to explode. Drag the selected slice away from center of pie.
Chart, format labels	EX 4.31	Select chart labels, then use Formatting toolbar to change font type, size, and style.
Chart, move	EX 4.11	Select the chart and drag it to a new location.
Chart, rotate a 3-D chart	EX 4.30	Select a 3-D chart. Click Chart, then 3-D View. Type the values you want in the Rotation and Elevation boxes.
Chart, select	EX 4.11	Click anywhere within the chart border. Same as activating.
Chart, update	EX 4.13	Enter new values in worksheet. Chart link to data is automatically updated.

TASK	PAGE #	RECOMMENDED METHOD
Chart, use picture	EX 4.36	Create column or bar chart. Select all columns/bars to be filled with picture, then click Insert, point to Picture, then click From File. Select picture from Insert Picture dialog box, then click OK.
Chart title, add or edit	EX 4.16	Select the chart. Click Chart, then click Chart Options. In the Titles tab, click one of the title text boxes, then type the desired title.
Chart Wizard, start	EX 4.07	Click ⊞.
Clipboard contents, paste into range	EX 2.15	Click ⊟.
Colors, apply to a range of cells	EX 3.24	*See* Reference Window: Applying Patterns and Color
Column width, change	EX 2.23	*See* Reference Window: Changing Column Width
Copy formula, use copy-and-paste method	EX 2.14	Select the cell with the formula to be copied, click ⊟, click the cell you want the formula copied to, then click ⊟.
Excel, exit	EX 1.34	Click File, then click Exit, or click the Excel Close button.
Excel, start	EX 1.05	Click the Start button, point to Programs, if necessary click Microsoft Office, and then click Microsoft Excel.
Font, select	EX 3.17	Select the cell or range you want to format. Click Format, click Cells, and then click the Font tab. Select the desired font from the Font List box.
Font, select size	EX 3.16	Select the cell or range you want to format. Click Format, click Cells, and then click the Font tab. Click the Font Size list arrow, then click the desired font size.
Footer, add	EX 2.32	In the Print Preview window, click Setup, then click the Header/Footer tab in the Page Setup dialog box. Click Custom Footer and edit the existing footer in the Footer dialog box.
Format, bold	EX 3.16	Select the cell or range you want to format, then click **B**, which toggles on and off.
Format, center in cell	EX 3.12	Select the cell or range you want to format. Click ☰, which toggles on and off.
Format, center text across columns	EX 3.14	Select the cell or range with text to center. Click Format, click Cells, then click the Alignment tab. Click the Horizontal Text alignment arrow and select Center Across Selection.
Format, comma	EX 3.11	Select the cell or range of cells you want to format, then click ☲.
Format, copy	EX 3.09	Select the cell or range of cells with the format you want to copy. Click ☑, then select the cell or range of cells you want to format.
Format, currency	EX 3.06	Select the cell or range of cells you want to format. Click Format, then click cells. Click the Number tab, click Currency in the Category box, then click the desired options.

TASK	PAGE #	RECOMMENDED METHOD
Format, font		Select the cell or range you want to format. Click the Font arrow and select the desired font.
Format, indent text	EX 3.15	Select the cell or range you want to indent. Click ▦.
Format, italic	EX 3.18	Select the cell or range you want to format, then click *I*, which toggles on and off.
Format, percent	EX 3.11	Select the cell or range of cells you want to format, then click %.
Format, wrap text	EX 3.13	Select the cell or cells you want to format. Click Format, click Cells, then click the Alignment tab. Click the Wrap text check box.
Formula, enter	EX 2.08	Click the cell in which you want the result to appear. Type = and then type the rest of the formula. For formulas that include cell references, type the cell reference or select each cell using the mouse or arrow keys. When the formula is complete, press Enter.
Formulas, display	EX 2.37	Click Tools, then click Options. Click the View tab, then click the Formulas check box.
Function, enter	EX 1.18	Type = to begin the function. Type the name of the function in either uppercase or lowercase letters, followed by an opening parenthesis. Type the range of cells you want to calculate using the function, separating the first and last cells in the range with a colon, as in B9:B15, or drag the pointer to outline the cells you want to calculate. *See also* Paste Function button, activate.
Gridlines, add or remove	EX 3.32	Click Tools, click Options, then click View. Click the Gridlines check box.
Header, add	EX 2.32	In the Print Preview window, click Setup, then click Header/Footer tab in the Page Setup dialog box. Click the Custom Header button to add a header in the Header dialog box.
Help, activate	EX 1.26	*See* Reference Window: Using the Office Assistant, and Figure 1-23
Labels, enter	EX 1.14	Select cell, then type text you want in cell.
Non-adjacent ranges, select	EX 4.25	Click the first cell or range of cells to select, then press and hold the Ctrl key as you select the other cell or range of cells to be selected. Release the Ctrl key when all non-adjacent ranges are highlighted.
Numbers, enter	EX 1.15	Select the cell, then type the number.
Paste Function button, activate	EX 2.19	*See* Reference Window: Using the Paste Function button
Patterns, apply to a range of cells	EX 3.24	*See* Reference Window: Applying Patterns and Color
Print Preview window, open	EX 2.30	Click ▣.
Printout, center	EX 2.31	In the Print Preview dialog box, click the Setup button. Click the Margins tab, then click the Horizontally and/or Vertically check boxes.

TASK	PAGE #	RECOMMENDED METHOD
Printout, landscape orientation	EX 3.34	In the Print Preview window, click the Setup button. Then click the Page tab in the Page Setup dialog box, then click the Landscape option button in the Orientation box.
Range, highlight	EX 1.30	Position pointer on the first cell of the range. Press and hold the mouse button and drag the mouse through the cells you want, then release the mouse button.
Range, move	EX 2.27	Select the cell or range of cells you want to move. Place the mouse pointer over any edge of the selected range until the pointer changes to an arrow. Click and drag the outline of the range to the new worksheet location.
Range, nonadjacent	EX 4.25	*See* Non-Adjacent ranges, select
Range, select	EX 1.30	*See* Range, highlight
Row or column, delete	EX 2.26	Click the heading(s) of the row(s) or column(s) you want to delete, click Edit, then click Delete.
Row or column, insert	EX 2.24	Click any cell in the row/column above which you want to insert the new row/column. Click Insert and then click Rows/Columns for every row/column in the highlighted range.
Sheet, activate	EX 1.10	Click the sheet tab for the desired sheet.
Sheet tab, rename	EX 2.15	Double-click the sheet tab for the desired sheet.
Shortcut menu, activate	EX 3.10	Select the cells or objects to which you want to apply the command, click the right mouse button, then select the command you want.
Spell check	EX 2.22	Click Tools, click Spelling.
Text box, add	EX 3.27	Click 📖 on the Drawing toolbar. Position pointer where text box is to appear, then click and drag to outline desired size and shape. Type comment in box.
Toolbar, add or remove	EX 3.26	Click any toolbar with right mouse button. Click the name of the toolbar you want to use/remove from the shortcut menu.
Undo button, activate	EX 2.26	Click ↰.
Workbook, open	EX 1.10	Click 📂 (or click File, then click Open). Make sure the Look in box displays the name of the folder containing the workbook you want to open, then click Open.
Workbook, save with a new name	EX 1.21	Click File, then click Save As. Change the workbook name as necessary. Specify the folder in which to save workbook in the Save in box. Click Save.
Workbook, save with same name	EX 1.21	Click 💾.
Worksheet, close	EX 1.33	Click File, then click Close, or click the worksheet Close button.
Worksheet, print	EX 1.31	Click 🖨 to print without adjusting any print options. Use the Print command on the File menu to adjust options.

File Finder

Location in Tutorial	Name and Location of Data File	Student Saves File As...	Student Creates File
EXCEL LEVEL 1, DISK 1			
Tutorial 1			
Session 1.1	Tutorial.01\Tutorial\Inwood.xls		
Session 1.2	Tutorial.01\Tutorial\Inwood.xls	Tutorial.01\Tutorial\Inwood 2.xls	
Review Assignments	Tutorial.01\Review\Inwood 3.xls	Tutorial.01\Review\Inwood 4.xls	
Case Problem 1	Tutorial.01\Cases\Enroll.xls	Tutorial.01\Cases\Enrollment.xls	
Case Problem 2	Tutorial.01\Cases\Budget.xls	Tutorial.01\Cases\BudgetSol.xls	
Case Problem 3	Tutorial.01\Cases\Medical.xls	Tutorial.01\Cases\Medical 2.xls	
Case Problem 4			Tutorial.01\Cases\CashCounter.xls
Tutorial 2			
Session 2.1			Tutorial.02\Tutorial\MSI Sales Report.xls
Session 2.2	Tutorial.02\Tutorial\MSI Sales Report.xls *(Saved from Session 2.1)*	Tutorial.02\Tutorial\Report.xls MSI Sales Report.xls	
Review Assignments	Tutorial.02\Review\MSI 1.xls	Tutorial.02\Review\	MSI Sales Report 2.xls
Case Problem 1			Tutorial.02\Cases\MJ Income.xls
Case Problem 2			Tutorial.02\Cases\Airline.xls
Case Problem 3	Tutorial.02\Cases\Fresh.xls	Tutorial.02\Cases\Fresh Air Sales Incentives.xls	
Case Problem 4			Tutorial.02\Cases\Portfolio.xls
Tutorial 3			
Session 3.1	Tutorial.03\Tutorial\Pronto.xls	Tutorial.03\Tutorial\ Pronto Salsa Company.xls	
Session 3.2	Tutorial.03\Tutorial\ Pronto Salsa Company.xls *(Saved from Session 3.1)*	Tutorial.03\Tutorial\ Pronto Salsa Company.xls	
Review Assignments	Tutorial.03\Review\Pronto 2.xls Tutorial.03\Review\Explore3.xls	Tutorial.03\Review\Pronto 3.xls Tutorial.03\Review\Pronto 4.xls Tutorial.03\Review\Explore3 Solution.xls	
Case Problem 1	Tutorial.03\Cases\Running.xls	Tutorial.03\Cases\Running2.xls	
Case Problem 2	Tutorial.03\Cases\Recycle.xls	Tutorial.03\Cases\Recycle2.xls Tutorial.03\Cases\Recycle Data.xls Tutorial.03\Cases\Recycle3.xls	
Case Problem 3	Tutorial.03\Cases\StateGov.xls	Tutorial.03\Cases\State Government.xls	
Case Problem 4			Tutorial.03\Cases\Payroll.xls
Tutorial 4			
Session 4.1	Tutorial.04\Tutorial\Concepts.xls	Tutorial.04\Tutorial\Cast Iron Concepts.xls	
Session 4.2	Tutorial.04\Tutorial\Cast Iron Concepts.xls *(Saved from Session 4.1)* Tutorial.04\Tutorial\Stove.pcx		
Review Assignments	Tutorial.04\Review\Concept2.xls Tutorial.04\Review\ ElectronicFilings.xls	Tutorial.04\Review\Cast Iron Concepts 2.xls Tutorial.04\Review\Filing Solution.xls	
Case Problem 1	Tutorial.04\Cases\Tekstar.xls	Tutorial.04\Cases\TekStar Electronics.xls	
Case Problem 2	Tutorial.04\Cases\DowJones.xls	Tutorial.04\Cases\Dow Jones Chart.xls Tutorial.04\Cases\Dow Jones 2.xls	
Case Problem 3	Tutorial.04\Cases\California.xls	Tutorial.04\Cases\California Economic Data.xls	
Case Problem 4			Tutorial.04\Cases\ RealtorCharts.xls